The Shared Heart

The Shared Heart

RELATIONSHIP
INITIATIONS
&
CELEBRATIONS

Joyce Vissell *RN, MS*   **Barry Vissell** *MD*

Foreword by Ram Dass

Printed in U.S.A. by Malloy Lithographing
First printing   Jan. 1984 5000
Second printing Nov. 1984 5000

Typeset by The Aptos Post

Library of Congress Catalog Card Number: 83-62976
ISBN: 0-9612720-0-7

ACKNOWLEDGEMENTS

The authors extend their heartfelt gratitude to Ram Dass for his love, support and criticism throughout the writing of this book; also to our editors, Susan Bagby and Michael Ellison; to Howard King and Larry Schmidt for their editorial comments; to Louise Wollenberg and Lorraine Rose for expert typing; to Patti Meyer, Liz Ellison, Joe Guido, Sandi Lynch, Helen Vissell, and Donna Sampson for proof-reading; to Jim Petersen for meticulous help in designing the book; and Nivedita, Rami, Robin Sale, Karl Jadrnicek, and Thomas Kirby for their loving artistic contributions.

A special appreciation goes to the many individuals and couples who supported and encouraged us, and who so openly shared the fears, hopes, pains, and joys they experienced on their journey toward oneness. These were the ones who brought the book to life.

May this book serve as an expression of appreciation for the help we have received from our teachers, especially those Blessed Ones who so gently and lovingly continue to guide us.

Contents

Illustrations

The Shared Heart

LOVE ONE ANOTHER

JESUS

Foreword

by RAM DASS

*But when two people are at one
in their inmost hearts,
They shatter even the strength
of iron or of bronze.
And when two people understand each other
in their inmost hearts,
Their words are sweet and strong
like the fragrance of orchids.*

EXCERPT FROM I-CHING

Here the I-Ching poetically points to the place of union between people where words cannot go. It is in such a union that two people realize that they are one...one which creatively manifests itself into myriad forms which dance with one another. This realization is the true marriage of the spirit.

For most of us earthly incarnates, we are imprisoned in our own separateness. But now and then, gracefully, we awaken to see that our prison is no more than the veils of mind, and that we have truly never been separate. For two people to recognize this together is to know one another in the most profound love.

Presently there are many two-person spiritual space-crafts floating about in which two beings throw in their lots together in order to enter into unitive love. It is suggested that while one person might remain asleep in the prison of mind, two people, helping each other as well as themselves, might be more likely to awaken and remain awake. Experience shows, however, that while two can help one another on the spiritual path, they also can conspire to create tougher prisons to escape from.

For this yoga of relationship to liberate rather than to entrap requires the deepest and most continuous "listening"... a listening

1

for the truth which, as the Tao Te Ching points out, "is seen only by eyes unclouded by longing". This truth must be recognized through the changing nature of forms.

Each of us exists simultaneously on many planes of reality. Even within one plane we have many social roles. Our awareness and resultant moment-to-moment identity moves from plane to plane, from role to role.

When we enter into a relationship with another similarly multifaceted being, in order for the relationship to remain relatively stable, secure, and efficient, we impose upon ourselves and each other the criterion of consistency. Thus we limit ourselves to one or perhaps two planes of consciousness and a few roles in order to be familiarly predictable, one to the other. Such requirements of consistency habituate and deaden us and move us further from that truth that is living spirit.

However, if we acknowledge living truth to be the criterion of an awakening relationship, then we meet in the midst of continuous change, in ourselves, in each other, and in the situation in which we find ourselves. Here we must be at home walking the fine line between cosmos and chaos. For this we must open once again to our "beginner's mind", to our deepest "listening", to our innocence. Two beings each contributing her or his own reawakened innocence to a shared cup is ecstasy — a source of healing and joy.

If two people are truly drawn to living spirit, then all that they share: love-making, changing diapers, periods of tense unspeaking silence, shared appreciations and meditations — all become grist for the mill of awakening. They are grateful for all of it, including the uniqueness of their partner, just as she or he is. Barry and Joyce are two such people. Their personal account reminds us of the gratefulness that attends this subtle seeking. They plough through the hard and soft spaces of the journey with great inner strength, deep respect for reflective inner tuning, and the trembling hearts of true *bhaktis*. Theirs is but one map of the journey of relationship. I know there will be many more maps in the future, for there are as many routes through relationship into unitive love as there are couples to make the journey.

Introduction

Dear Brothers and Sisters on the path of love:

Some years ago we attended a meditation seminar with a well-known teacher. After a lovely weekend of inspiration, instruction, and practice, time was allowed for questions and answers. No one asked about meditation. No one asked about spiritual practices. One person after another asked about the relationship process. What emerged was a mass of confusion about how to reconcile deep, committed love relationships while following the path of consciousness.

This book is intended as a guide for those who desire personal relationships. But more than this, it is a guide for those of us who want our relationships to serve as vehicles for our spiritual awakening. This book is for those of us with the sincerity and courage to look at our desires, fears, anger — our full human condition. For as we accept our humanity with love and compassion, so will we also open our hearts to that which is more than human in us. As we embrace, rather than hate, our limitations, we find ourselves embracing our perfection as well.

This book is for those of us who are learning the beauty and power of the monogamous or committed relationship. For the deeper we go with one other person, the more we learn about ourselves. In addition, the less we hide in ourselves, the more our heart is available to others, and the deeper our capacity for joy.

We all long for love. At the same time, we are all afraid of what true love requires. To merge into unity, to share at the deepest level of being with another person, requires detachment from our ego-natures — the letting go of all we think we are. There can be no real relationship of love without this surrender. We often find that we can't have our way and have love too. We're afraid of surrender because we don't understand what it really is. Some of us see it as a void, an emptiness, a powerless nonexistence. Some fear losing our will and being dominated or controlled by another.

There are times for every couple when one of us is convinced

3

of being right and the other wrong, and we feel miles apart in the same room. For one of us to give in under those circumstances seems like throwing our very life away. When we do surrender at times like this and risk the very worst, we become filled with peace and joy. What we were holding onto seems so trivial, like a speck of dirt. Instantly the miles dissolve, and the mask we had projected onto our partner's face disappears, revealing our hidden lover, revealing that enchantingly beautiful essence of being that is both of us, that is love personified, that is God.

This is how it is for so many of us. We're caught desperately fighting for a speck of dirt, feeling our whole world depends on it, while we miss out on the vastness of love so patiently waiting for our open heart.

Every deep love relationship is a path of initiation, a journey involving many tests and trials. In our longing for love, for the omnipresent perfection which is God, life provides us with numerous opportunities for growth and advancement. The deeper the relationship, the more imperfection is brought to the surface. The deeper our longing for love, the more light floods our being, and the dark shadows of fear, doubt, pride, anger, jealously, greed (and many others) emerge for their last stand. They are exposed by our desire for truth, and then transfigured by the light of love.

A deep relationship is like a hot fire. When we focus upon power, or domination, or excitement, or sensory pleasures, we get burned. When we focus upon sincerely learning about love, when we desire to use our relationship as a way to come to God, then the fire will consume the dross, the negativity, and leave pure gold — our shining essence.

In our classes, workshops, and counseling sessions, we have found that sharing our experiences and initiations, our failures as well as our successes, was very helpful to people. As a result, this book contains many personal anecdotes, as well as case-studies/stories of couples to illustrate the various themes. A deep learning can take place through identification in the process of story-telling.

We want this book to be very practical and informative, as well as inspiring. Many of the chapters end with a guided meditation or exercise which evolved from our classes and other work with couples. Our greatest hope is to provide you with useful tools for the initiations which face you on the relationship journey.

Writing has been an entire initiation in itself for us. This book was conceived in the stillness of meditation, in the Presence of

God. We recognized and acknowledged our utter helplessness to manifest our vision by ourselves without relying on Divine Help. Then time after time we would get side-tracked into thinking *we* were writing the book. The book would become number one, God number two. Then we would wonder why words never got onto paper. Or if words did get written, they would get thrown out later. Only when we again humbled ourselves, recognizing the true love, wisdom, and power of the universe, were we free to serve others with our words.

This is perhaps the greatest lesson of the relationship process. We all so easily get side-tracked, making our relationship more important than God. If we could share the deepest truth we know concerning love relationships, it would be this: *There is only one love relationship, the bond between the outer personality and the Inner Beingness, the bond between the soul and the Spirit, the human and the Divine.* Our relationships with others are manifestations and reflections of this One Relationship. We can either get lost in the reflections, or we can see "through the mirror," using our relationships as vehicles on the highway to the Source of All.

We started writing this book when we conceived our second child. Now that our little Mira is nearing two years old we are able to look back over the incredible trials and initiations we went through with each chapter as it was written. Finishing the manuscript has been the hardest part, for one can never be finished with a topic so vast as the love relationship.

Several months ago we rented a friend's cabin on the wintery slopes of Mt. Shasta in Northern California. Much of the inspiration for this book came to us while meditating on this mountain, which has been held sacred down through the centuries. Here we hoped to regain inspiration for the last thrust of the book. However, this was to be a different kind of trip. Mira was teething, didn't like the cabin, and cried and complained much of the time. By the end of our stay we were weary and our writing tablets were blank. Sitting outside for a moment alone, we felt discouraged and said a prayer for help. The reply lovingly came through us both: *We are not only to write a book on love, we are to become all that we are writing.* Holding a crying baby late in the night was our work on the book. When we could do that with joy and thankfulness in our hearts, the book could then continue. So it is in every relationship. As we can accept with thankfulness the trials and initiations that come, so will our love continue to grow.

Through this book we offer you the fruits of nineteen years of loving each other and ten years of guiding couples through their own initiations. We hope these thoughts, feelings and stories awaken your hearts to your own inner knowledge, and the ideal of the love relationship. As we all strive to be pure love, to become all we are intended to be, we are helping to spread the light of consciousness and serve humanity. May your heart be opened to the truth within you.

Joyce and Barry Vissell
Aptos, California
Spring, 1983

one

Soulmates

Harmony is the law of love.

SAINT GERMAIN

...if you were to define love, the only word big enough to engulf it all would be "life." Love is life in all of its aspects. And if you miss love, you miss life. Please don't.

LEO BUSCAGLIA

Imagine being separated from your beloved for eighteen years!

Sometimes in meditation I glimpse my life before coming to earth to incarnate in this body. As I feel this, Barry is always with me and I know we have been together in a deep and beautiful way before entering these bodies. It is as if it was decided that we make the journey toward earth at the same time. I was born May 18, 1946, in Buffalo, New York, second child of a Protestant family. Barry was born nine days later in Brooklyn, New York, second child of a Jewish family. Before we were born, I feel there was a promise that we would be reunited when the time was right...and only when the time was right.

When I was an adolescent I suffered the usual pains of loneliness. I was not the type of girl that was asked out on many dates. I was rather proper and shy in my behavior with boys. Weekend nights were spent with my beloved family or babysitting. Sometimes I would cry late at night because there was no special friend in my life. During these moments of great loneliness I would feel a comforting presence come and tell me that there was someone waiting for me. I would then get an image of a tall, dark-haired man, who was a doctor. This image would come to me perhaps once a week.

When I was eighteen I went to Hartwick College, a small Lutheran School in upstate New York. The population was predominantly Protestant, and I held a secret hope in my heart that I would meet a nice man of my religion and perhaps we would marry. Barry, meanwhile, had applied to several prestigious colleges and had been rejected by them all. It was then too late to apply to any more schools, and he had nowhere to go.

One day, in the midst of his moping about at his high school, he was called to the school office. There, a representative of Hartwick College who had somehow heard of his plight, had an application already filled out. He described the school in roughly five minutes, and asked Barry if he would like to sign and make it final. Without a moment's hesistation, Barry signed the application. As I look back now, I realize how little we are aware of the divine hand working in our lives, and how little we understand all that is done to bring us together, to help us all fulfill our destinies here on earth.

How romantic it was to meet during a snow-ball fight between dorms, and to be smashed in the face with snow by your life-time partner! Then there was a movie, and walking back to the dorm, a kiss. That kiss was like the kiss upon Sleeping Beauty, and something surged through us both, awakening each to a deeper place within. We were but children in terms of our maturity, yet for an instant we gazed into each other's eyes and remembered our deep and eternal love. Though it would be years until that happened again, we could never forget the memory, though at times we tried very hard to.

As innocent children we probed our way into the mysteries of love. We used to meet secretly every evening in the dining room and talk for hours. We had much catching up to do! Finally, I felt I had met someone who understood me completely and was my best friend.

The day came, however, that Barry told me he was Jewish and could never marry outside of his religion. I was shocked! How could he be Jewish in this Protestant school? Of course we couldn't marry. We really should break the relationship. But we were hooked and love pulled us higher and higher, though like caught fish, we struggled more and more. I transferred to a different college in order to be away from him. He also transferred to a more Jewish-populated school, hoping to meet a Jewish girl. At Columbia Presbyterian Medical Center I thought for sure I would meet that tall doctor of my vision.

Barry and I couldn't keep apart, of course, and we kept visiting each other. The love grew and grew, and our fights got worse and worse. We each wanted the other to change religion, to make it alright somehow. Finally we decided to break up completely and not see each other ever again. It seemed like the only thing to do, as neither would change for the other. Our family and friends were happy and thought we had acted wisely. We, however, were miserable.

One dark and lonely night I took the elevator to the 20th floor of my dorm building. Stepping out onto the roof, I beheld the entire panorama of New York City. I cried bitterly and prayed to God in the way I had been taught at church. I told God I was breaking up with Barry for Him and asked if this was right. I prayed for a sign to help me understand.

The next day a friend of mine got a surprise visit from her mother, whom I loved very much. She told me that the night before she felt a definite impulse to give me a little poem from her prayer book. She gave me the poem, and one sentence was underlined,

"Above all else Love is most important."

A current went through me and I knew love surpassed personalities, religions, doctrines, everything. I ran to the phone and called Barry. He understood. Shortly thereafter we were engaged to be married. The two struggling fish had surrendered to love and were being pulled in. I was reunited with the tall, dark-haired doctor-to-be of my vision.

Barry and I had found out the hard way that one's life partner cannot be picked out by the intellect, the shoulds and the should-nots of an upbringing, or the desires of the mind and the body. Only the heart, only love, can tell. What seems to the mind as the

greatest obstacle, through the healing power of love, can become the greatest strength. When we thought of marriage, the difference in religious upbringing seemed insurmountable. Yet through love, patience, and understanding, our path to God has become universal, and is certainly the greatest strength in our life together. We have seen this happen with many couples. An obstacle will present itself in the merging process and, rather than giving up, if the couple works through the barrier they come out on the other side much stronger and wiser because of it. It is as if the barriers were there purposefully to make the love between the couple deeper and more beautiful. When they manifest themselves, they are gifts, which, when surmounted, serve as stepping stones to bring a couple closer in realization of God.

In wanting to be with one's life partner it is best not to think about how you want him or her to be like, but rather, to feel in your heart how much you already love this person. It is this love going forth that will draw the person to you. The mind is a poor judge of who is right. A little story which illustrates this comes to mind:

Once, when Barry and I first started counseling in Santa Cruz, we saw a divorced woman in her forties who became especially dear to our hearts. She had grown children and now was alone and wanted very much to be with a man. Month after month we would hear of her struggle with different men. The right one just never seemed to manifest. During one session she was particularly discouraged and we asked her to describe just what type of man she was wanting. She was quick to reply and listed about ten practical qualifications, such as same age, grown children, stable income, etc. We then suggested sitting together and picturing a man of these qualifications coming into her life.

As soon as I closed my eyes the face of a man popped into my mind. This was a man we knew very well from past counseling experiences, and yes, he fit all the qualifications. I decided I would not tell Barry or the woman. That night Barry described the exact same person, vision, and experience. We wondered for a long time whether to introduce them. Matching up clients seemed highly unprofessional so we decided to try to forget we had seen the man's face so vividly. Besides we hadn't seen him in over a year and did not know how to get in touch with him anyway, so it seemed easy to just forget it.

The very next day we traveled to San Francisco for a seminar. As we walked in the door, the first person we met was the man of our vision. Barry was totally surprised by the "coincidence" that he blurted out the whole story. When we described the woman to him he became very excited.

We had them both come to our home to meet, which was an awkward moment for everyone. This man had all the qualifications that our client-friend thought she wanted, and vice-versa. They later dated each other twice and found they had a great deal in common. However, a certain quality of the heart was missing, that indefinable spark was not there. After two meetings they chose to stop seeing each other.

The four of us learned so much from that experience. Only your heart can tell your life partner. Only your heart can draw that being to you. Your mind will naturally seek the easiest person to be with, one with whom it is easy and comfortable. But your heart, the voice of the soul, will seek the person who can best help you climb toward God. *The mind seeks an easy relationship. The heart seeks a spiritual partner.* Many people are married to their perfect spiritual partner and do not even realize it because their mind and desires are wanting the relationship to be more comfortable and painless. *Many times the difficulty with your partner is the very thing compelling your spiritual development.* It takes a lot of love poured forth to either feel your spiritual partner or draw him or her to you. What beautiful work!

> *...Love is a fruit in season at all times, and within reach of every hand. Anyone may gather it and no limit is set. Everyone can reach this love through meditation, spirit of prayer and sacrifice, by an intense inner life.*
>
> MOTHER TERESA

I remember my struggle before accepting Joyce as my spiritual partner. From the very beginning of our relationship, even before we met, there was a definite place of "knowing" deep within myself; so deep, however, that it was easily buried by my conscious desires and mind.

As an eighteen-year-old first-year college student, I was what you might call a late bloomer. A very awkward, shy, and sensitive child, I was much more interested in sports than girls. Much the same as Joyce, I didn't take notice of the other sex until I was almost eighteen years old. In my last year of high school, I experienced two brief, but intense romances. I was very awkward, and I believe I scared both girls away.

In college I tried (for a few months anyway) to polish my act. I somehow fell in with a certain infamous fraternity. At the time I tried to convince myself that sophisticated girls were the ones to be with. The word in 1964 was "cool" (you know, not like one's mother). This quest was a failure from the start.

One day I was sitting with my "cool" friends at a soccer game in the very cold late autumn of Oneonta, New York, when I saw Joyce for the first time. She didn't attract me in the way I thought I was supposed to be attracted. She was sitting on the bleachers above me and off to the side, laughing and joking with a group of boys and girls. She was acting silly and having a great time. And I remember, as if it were yesterday, my feeling of attraction for her. Her joy was innocently and unselfconsciously bubbling over. It was very infectious, but somehow made me feel very serious at the time. She wasn't doing any of the things I would have wanted her to do. Yet, there was a feeling of insecurity deep inside me...that this girl would never willingly have much to do with me.

Then came the fateful snow-ball fight with my well-aimed snow-ball. Later we were assigned to be waiter and waitress together in the dining hall. How beautifully God works!

Finally, I got up my nerve and asked Joyce out on a date to see the new movie "Tom Jones" several evenings away. The day of the movie came, and I bumped into Joyce walking on campus. She asked me, "What time will you be picking me up for our date tonight?" With a perfect deadpan expression I replied, "What date?" She got visibly flustered. I started laughing, and it was almost the end of a relationship that hadn't yet started. However, she finally did see the humor of the situation...I think.

Well, I did in fact pick her up that evening. Our first date! We started walking down the hill through the campus. We had problems right from the start. Joyce had a way of walking that was the antithesis of the way I wanted a woman to walk. She had a kind of childlike bounce to her step...really enjoying just being alive and walking. Unfortunately I could not appreciate that at the time. I was just plain embarrassed. Slowly widening the space between us, I hoped nobody would notice we were together.

Yet it was our good-night kiss that evening that really put me into a turmoil. It was truly the kiss of death, because from that moment on, all that was false in me started to die. I would lay awake at night in my dorm room struggling with my conflicting feelings about this girl named Joyce. I felt so at home, so at peace in her presence. I just couldn't let go of how "unsuitable" she was for me, and my mind-set about who was right for me and who wasn't. I continued to struggle with her physical appearance, which seemed far from my late-teenage ideals. Today it seems rather silly, but at the time it was dreadfully important and caused me much suffering.

There were also many "little" things in her personality that turned me off. Finally, however, the day came when I found out she wasn't Jewish. It seemed a final confirmation of all my doubts. She didn't really look Jewish, but her last name of Wollenberg fooled me. But by then it was too late. I had tasted of the love far beyond my little head-trips. Try as I did to push Joyce out of my mind and heart, I could not keep the longing to be with her submerged. It would inevitably bubble up reminding me of that heavenly wine which would then all but drive me crazy.

In those early days, we would get together because the pull was so great, and there would be a moment of near ecstasy. Then our minds and egos would pull us back down, and we would sadly realize that we really shouldn't be together. Sometimes we would fight and argue, blaming and trying to change each other. I smile now when I remember the many, many "scenes" outside her dorm, while everyone was watching Barry and Joyce go at it again.

This whole time, imperceptably, the false was dying and truth was growing within each of us. After each fight, and I was again alone righteously proclaiming to myself how unworkable our relationship was, I would start to suffer a loss of something. I would find myself in a state of mourning. The grievances I was holding onto would lose power and importance — and die a little more. Joyce was becoming more and more attractive to me. Her beauty seemed to be emerging and a respect for her was growing within me.

Perhaps every couple has at least one seemingly insurmountable barrier. Ours at the time, and for the first four years we knew each other, was our religious upbringing. Religious differences seem more easily worked through in this day and age than what Joyce and I went through in the mid-sixties. It is not that I was a particularly devout Jew, nor Joyce a devout Protestant. It was more of a cultural shock for both of us. In both our families it was simply unheard of for anyone to marry outside of the religion. These traditional values had a lot of power and hold on us. The question, "And how will the children be raised?", would echo in our minds.

It was, in the end, fine for Joyce to stay Protestant and me Jewish, but it seemed at the time that if our children were neither of the two they would be nothing — they would lack spiritual direction.

It's true! This was a major stumbling block in our lives at the time, and the source of many arguments. But, as one of our teachers later reminded us, "Your greatest weakness will turn out to be your greatest strength." As a couple, this was our greatest weakness, and we were forced to go deeper into our respective religions. And the deeper we went, the more we felt the common source of all religions: the spirit of love! We discovered that all the differences between religions existed only in the mind. And the mind has only the concept of love, whereas the heart experiences it.

Our greatest weakness has indeed become our greatest strength. For the all-prevailing spirit of love and truth has become the center of our relationship and family, our ever-present orientation.

This is the heart of the whole issue of soulmates, or twin souls, or twin flames, or whatever you want to call it. Too many people are running around looking for "that perfect partner"...*outside of themselves*. All of the esoteric terms and definitions tend to put most people more in their heads and less in their hearts. The true soulmate is a state of consciousness, not a person. You may even be with your perfect mate and dislike each other intensely, failing one of the main tests of your life.

The purpose of a love relationship is to set your sights on love, rather than the relationship. The test of every marriage is to come to love love, more than to love the person. That love comes from your heart, the deepest center of your being. Love is a feeling, a radiation of light, a presence. It is not a personality. When you touch upon love, you are touching your soulmate — and soul-marriage — the mystical marriage. It all happens within you, the merging of your soul with your spirit, the merging of who you thought you were with who you really are. In this realm of the heart you then see with the eyes of God. All things and persons are seen for what they are — *light-infused and love-permeated*. Your husband or wife glows with a beauty that can make you gasp!

Can you see this? Can you understand the words of Jesus, "Seek ye first the Kingdom, and all things will be added unto you."? All the prophets and masters say the same thing: when God becomes number one in your life, when the indwelling spirit becomes more important than the who's and what's and where's, your life then becomes a flow of perfection. Then you create beauty in all that you see, hear, touch, or in any way turn your attention upon. Love is never-ending creation.

My heart has become an ocean, beloved,
since You have poured Your love into it.

HAZRAT INAYAT KHAN

Whenever Barry and I ponder the issue of soulmates and the tendency we all have to look outside of ourselves for fulfillment, we are reminded of a very powerful experience I had. It was actually a turning point in my life.

In the summer of 1978 we decided that to truly advance on the spiritual path we had to submit ourselves to a series of strict disciplines. We were at the stage where we thought we had to go somewhere and do something. We decided upon a very intensive six-week retreat. We rented a large house outside the town of Mt. Shasta in Northern California. One of our objectives was to work with our sexual energy, which at times flowed so powerfully between us that we seemed to have little control over it. Our plan was to sleep in separate bedrooms and abstain from sex, which proved to be very interesting. We also decided to spend at least half of our time in silence, and totally alone. Every other day one of us could watch Rami while the other went to meditate on the slopes of Mt. Shasta.

About one week after our arrival we were sufficiently settled into our new location to start. I'll never forget my first day alone. I had looked forward to it for many weeks. After Rami nursed in the morning, I left her in the capable hands of Barry and drove up the mountain. This was my first full day away from Rami since her birth fifteen months ago, and that alone was an amazing feeling. Walking through Panther Meadows I felt the strong Presence of Divine Mother — the female aspect of God. I sat by a rock overlooking the bubbly stream and looked at all the wild-flowers growing everywhere. In that moment I felt Rami so strongly and felt that her presence in my life allowed me to feel the Divine Mother. By caring for Rami, I was growing closer and closer to that mother-presence within me. I felt so grateful for Rami and the privilege of motherhood. That moment will always be very precious to me.

Afterwards, I chose a place and forced myself to meditate for six hours, doing various breathing and other practices. In my zeal to reach that state of complete inner calm I neglected to also be conscious of flowing in my body, and ended up with a great big headache. So much for my first day on "the intensive retreat."

The next day with Rami was very joyful, and the following day alone was more balanced than the first. On the fourth day Barry took off for the mountain bright and early. Rami and I both had a difficult day. She was having trouble cutting teeth and I was having trouble with myself. I was beginning to feel overwhelmed with loneliness. I had spoken to no one in four days except for Rami, whose vocabulary consisted of "Mama, Barry, Dolly." She cried a lot over her teeth, while my mind was crying a lot within. Doubts came crashing in: "What a stupid thing to be doing. It's not right that you don't see Barry and sleep with him. This is getting you nowhere, needless suffering..." On and on the doubts and negativity came. Rami finally settled down for the night and I went to my lonely room downstairs. I felt lonelier than I had in a long while. At that point, our VW van pulled up and out jumped Barry. He was shining like the sun and I could tell he had a good day from the way he walked. I watched him sadly as he ascended the outside steps to his private bedroom. My mind and body were aching to be with him. He had been my best friend for thirteen years and I knew just being with him for a few minutes would lift the loneliness I was feeling. I was ready to run out the door, but when I turned to my heart the answer was: "No, do not go, continue to be alone!"

With much sadness I went out into the evening air and started to walk. The darkness seemed blacker than usual and even the presence of my beloved dog, Bokie, didn't cheer me up. I felt indescribable loneliness and such a strong desire to be with a friend. Tears flowed from my eyes as I cried out to God for help to understand. In that moment I was filled with the feeling of being with my very best friend. It was as if that friend surrounded me everywhere and talked with me and walked with me and loved me totally. Yet I was alone. I knew in that moment that my truest friend is within. When I look only to Barry for that friendship...or to Rami...or to any other human being, I will never be totally satisfied. It is the friend within our own heart that fills the loneliness and gives us the feeling of being totally loved. The more we contact and feel our inner friend, the more we can give and receive from others. The highest work we can do in a relationship is to seek the joy and stillness of this Inner Presence and then share that love with others. I forget this over and over again and allow myself to get far away. But when I do remember and feel this great indwelling God Presence, then peace and gratitude flood my being.

The lover who leans upon the beloved's response, his love is like the flame that needs oil to live; but the lover who stands on his own feet is like the lantern of the sun that burns without oil.

HAZRAT INAYAT KHAN

two

The Freed Need Seeds

Joy, joy, joy
You've brought me so much joy.
I never knew how to love before
You taught me to be me,
You taught me to be free.

A SONG GIVEN TO JOYCE
IN A DREAM

It was autumn, 1974, and Joyce and I were staying with friends in the San Francisco Bay area. We were struggling with the decision of where to live, though we sensed the direction our lives were taking and the work we were eventually to do together. To help the decision, one day we set out by car to explore the area north of San Francisco. We ended up lost on some winding mountain road that finally plunged to the coast. There in front of us appeared a sign saying "Sea Ranch." Something about that name clicked with me, and intuitively I opened my little blue address book. There I found a list of names and addresses given us by a special friend and teacher. On the list was a well-known and loved teacher, who was living at Sea Ranch, Ca. We had heard about this man who had taken a vow of silence many years ago, and had a strong desire to meet him. We felt this was our chance — we would just drop in on him. In our innocence we did not realize the task ahead of us.

We somehow made it to the administrative office of Sea Ranch and announced that we were here to see the well-known teacher. First, the woman said she was not allowed to give directions without authorization. After much convincing, however, she finally called the house. Then there were more delays, and more questioning, and finally we were given directions and told we could only stay a few minutes, that he was in seclusion.

Off we went, slightly dazed and not a little apprehensive about what we were getting into. We approached the house, which commanded a beautiful view of the ocean, perched on the top of a small cliff. We were greeted at the door warmly, but again told we should not stay long. Then we were shown into a bedroom where the teacher was sitting on his bed writing a letter. He motioned us to sit on the bed with him.

We arranged ourselves comfortably and soon felt entirely at ease, as if we were sitting in the presence of a child rather than a middle-aged man. We were laughing and having a jolly time, then suddenly he looked — or better "tuned-in" — to my unadorned left ring-finger. He then looked at Joyce's finger, with a ring on it, and again deliberately back at mine. Immediately, his chalk clicked against the slate, producing the following:

"Where's your ring?"

"Oh, packed away somewhere, I think," was my reply.

"Why aren't you wearing it?", next appeared on the slate.

Still confident I listed my reasons:

"I've never been able to wear rings."

"It's uncomfortable."

"It gets caught on things."

None of this appeared to convince him, and I started to feel uncomfortable and defensive. I glanced over at Joyce who was smiling at me, but obviously in agreement with this stranger.

Cornered, I made a final, somewhat desperate attempt.

"I really tried wearing it for quite a while. But one day, while meditating in a slightly darkened room with a stick of incense burning near me, I reached for something and caught the burning tip of the incense under my ring." I became dramatic, waving my hands, "Frantically I tried to get it out, helplessly feeling my flesh burning. That did it. From then on I stopped wearing my ring."

There followed a long moment of silence. He smiled, looked at me with deepest love, and wrote on the chalkboard:

"You need her more than she needs you."

Suddenly I felt like a balloon with a critical air leak. Yet at the same time it was indescribably wonderful to be exposed — not having to hide. I felt something in me wake up. A scene flashed before my inner eyes that had taken place some years before. It was in the late winter of 1972 in Los Angeles. I was finishing medical school at the University of Southern California. It was a rather turbulent time for our relationship. I was on one of my kicks of asserting my independence, acting like I didn't need anyone or anything. Joyce was polarized to the other side, feeling insecure, weak, and over-dependent. Recent "friends" were all eager to agree with this illusion. I had begun training with the Gestalt Therapy Institute of L.A., a good experience in many ways, but it also provided food for my "independence ego-trip."

The cork finally exploded from this bottle, Thank God. I foolishly tried to prove my independence by having an affair with another woman. Joyce decided to leave. It took a few days for me to realize she was really gone, but I still held on to my rightness, while slipping deeper and deeper into depression. I meandered about the hospital like a robot, and isolated myself from everyone. This went on for about a week, and might have continued, were it not for the help of a friend...and a mind-shattering experience.

One evening, all my feelings started to come to the surface, especially unbearable despair. All this was very new to me, but I had no time to think about what was happening. I was lying on the floor in a pitiful heap, sobbing uncontrollably. Then suddenly, a word started to emerge from my depths, and soon I was calling out, "mama...ma...ma"! I was an infant, helpless. I didn't know where my mother was, but I needed her terribly. I could see my own mother's face, how she looked when I was an infant. Then I saw Joyce's face, blended with my mother's. I never knew I needed them...so much. However, the feeling transcended my mother and wife. I was pouring my heart out to the Cosmic Mother, although years had to pass for me to realize what had transpired.

I was never able to be the same person as before. The process of awakening my feminine half, the integration of male-female energies, had begun. I realized then, my relationship with Joyce would lead me to this point faster than anything else. I knew I needed her — physically, emotionally, mentally, and spiritually.

Soon after this experience, Joyce returned having regained a sense of strength deep within her. Another door had opened between the two of us leading to a new level of commitment and love.

The words on the teacher's chalkboard, and the vision of the Los Angeles experience, had a profound effect on me. It has always been easier for Joyce to come to me with a problem, but harder for me to ask her for help. Although we have always needed each other equally, I was suppressing my awareness of need. I had made my need and dependence into a monster, something evil. Unconsciously, therefore, it exerted great influence over my life. In this sense, the teacher was right. Because of the power I had blindly given this "monster" of need, I *was* needing Joyce more than she needed me.

In the years that followed these experiences, this monster has been turning out to be my best friend. My acceptance and love of my human needs has opened my heart to my spiritual needs. Unless we learn to respect our full human condition, with all our limitations, how can we respect our Divine Condition? It's like trying to appreciate the fragrance of a flower while disliking its appearance. They can't be separated. If we do separate them, we miss out on both.

How can we learn to transform need? To answer this, it might be helpful to look at the different manifestations of need in our relationships. In truth, we have only one need: the need for God, the Spirit of Divine Love. This one need, however, may be expressed on four levels in the human relationship: physical, emotional, mental, and spiritual. In other words, the four elemental levels of being have four levels of need and dependence.

Let's start with physical need in the relationship: the needs of our body. This corresponds to our dependence on the earth element, which nurtures us and provides us with food. We acknowledge our other physical needs, but how often do we forget that our bodies need to be touched, nurtured, and loved? As long as we have a body, its sensual needs must be respected — but not over-indulged. Like a child, our body needs love and appreciation — and also firm discipline.

In our relationships we constantly face the choice of what to do with this physical need. We can either "go to sleep," suppressing this need, or we can stay awake, allowing ourselves to keep in touch with it. At times it is *so* easy to lose ourselves in complete identification with our bodies. At other times we so easily repress our sensual need, forgetting to respect our bodies. The topic of sex is so charged with emotion, and often so subtle, that real sensitivity is required to work with it consciously. If we're to live in real love, the sexual part of our relationship must be transformed — must be raised out of the darkness into the light.

The second level of need or dependence between the couple is emotional, linked with the element of water. It is here where people drown themselves, where unresolved and repressed feelings from the past surface at the most inopportune times, threatening to dominate the relationship. Every committed couple knows the force of the waves of anger, the currents of jealousy, the thick fogs of doubt, the downpour of tears, and the whirlpools of fear. In time, all can know the crystal-clear, shining waters of Divine Love.

We have to learn to see and respect our emotional need for each other, the often subtle ways we lean on our partners. For a long time I felt that Joyce and I leaned on each other too much, that it was unhealthy, that we were stifling each other. It made me feel awful. Emotional dependence had become a negative entity.

My Los Angeles experience showed me that emotional need has higher dimensions. Rather than pretending to be strong and independent, we can find our true strength by freely admitting our human emotional need. The real humble person is not afraid of dependence, but on the contrary, enjoys it. We come to realize how deep is our need for God — not some abstract up-in-the-sky God, but God manifest in all creation. A disciple once asked his teacher to help him feel his need for God. The teacher took him down to the river and pushed the student's head under water. After a very long time the disciple came up sputtering and gasping for air. "When you need God," the teacher said, "the same way you are needing to breath right now, then your search will be over."

The need of a couple for each other is one manifestation of the need for God. When we see emotional dependence in this way, we finally stop struggling and surrender to *Who* we really need. We don't say, "Aha, I don't need you. I only need God," and then run off to be alone. We can stay right there and enjoy our need for our partner as an expression of our need for the All, the Everything.

Likewise, just because we accept our emotional dependence, we have no right to demand that our needs be met by our loved one. We often try to do this, but it never works. No individual is obligated to fulfill our needs. It is enough to open our hearts to our dependence. This simple yet courageous act instantly fills us with all that we need.

Mastery of the emotions does not happen by force. It is not something we can subdue. But by loving acceptance we can rise above all human emotion. This is what Jesus demonstrated by walking on the water.

Next comes mental need, corresponding to the element of air. This is the realm of communication, ideas, and creativity. Every couple has at some time had a *real* conversation where two minds become one, where the mental activity of both is raised, focused, and insight after insight emerges. This is so much more than a talk. It is every bit as intimate as the sexual experience.

Although these "talks" are often spontaneous, we need to be reminded that conscious preparation can help them to occur. We can listen to a favorite piece of music, read out loud to each other from an inspiring book, or just sit together in silence, asking that our minds be used as instruments of truth. The ways are many. Unfortunately, couples rarely allow the time to prepare for deeper conversation. We too often spend our precious time together bouncing mundane thoughts off each other, ignoring our need for "fresh air," a creative mental exchange.

Yet when we realize our true mental needs, we do anything we can to start this process. Once started, our dialogue can draw inspiration from a very high level of consciousness, and supply the food required by an evolving relationship. A couple can become one person talking with two mouths, where there can be neither defensiveness nor sense of separateness. Problem areas of weakness or hurt can be exposed with a sense of lightness, allowing the air to be cleared. As a couple we can create new ways of being. We can shape our very destinies. We can think with the mind of God, and see with the eyes of God. We can glimpse the vision of how beautifully and perfectly our lives and relationship are unfolding. We can stand back and admire the intricate patterns in our life's tapestry, where the individual stitching mistakes not only appear small, but are so easily corrected as well.

A couple once came to us for counseling. They were obviously in love although in a somewhat youthful way. We quickly sensed two things about them: First, that many tests lay ahead of them which would deepen their joy and peace; and second, we sensed the presence of that inner connection which seems to come from true lovers — not just two people in love, but a couple that has a definite service to perform together in the world.

However, they still had much work to do to clear away the negativity which was blocking this higher work. A prominent aspect of this negativity had to do with need and dependence. The man was more sensitive and introverted than most men, and was very aware of his dependence upon his wife. She was less in touch with her need, outwardly taking on the social butterfly role — free, light, and independent. This threw them out of balance, both equally playing a part. The superficial observer might think, "What is she doing with *him*!" Certainly, in each of their minds a similar question had at times been phrased. They had both agreed at some level that he needed her more. In their mutual insecurity she unconsiously acted out the butterfly and he the slug — heavy, slow, and somewhat sticky!

In reality, their level of consciousness was equal, and so too their level of need. Both were equally sharing a negative, one-sided image of dependence. The woman had disassociated herself from her need, which caused her to act out the "butterfly." The man, with his ever-present awareness of his need, was overindulging his feelings while at the same time being ashamed of them. They were polarized on two extremes of the spectrum of need. It's remarkable how one extreme sustains the other. The more she denies her dependence, the more dependent he acts. The "stickier" he gets, the harder the "butterfly" flaps her wings. It takes two to play this game — and only one to stop it.

Working with this couple was not difficult. Their love and sincerity opened the door for the needed help. Our work as therapists was to see past the superficial game and say as little as possible. By themselves they came to the realization of their equally-shared need.

Finally we come to the greatest need that exists in a relationship of love: the spiritual need, linked with the element of fire. It is when a couple, after many tests and initiations, comes to that deep inner knowing that they cannot realize God separate from each other. There comes a time along the path of love when we are faced with our own selfishness, and the many subtle ways we compete with our mates. As long as our dreams and goals are more important to us than those of our partner, we prevent ourselves from experiencing Divine Love. Unconditional love is attained the moment we forget ourselves and truly desire to help another on this

journey of life. This is similar to the Bodhisattva vow in Buddhism — the vow of selflessness and service, knowing this is the way of illumination.

It can also be said that the ultimate need of a couple is for the "mystical marriage," the integration of the male and female sides within each person. This is the fulfillment of a relationship, and is accelerated by the relationship process itself. What we really see in our loved one — what we really are attracted to — is what we have not yet opened to in ourself. The beauty and wholeness which has always been within us we first project onto our beloved. Then we yearn to be with our beloved and enter full-swing into the cosmic dance of relationship. Finally, the dance awakens us to the remembrance of our original wholeness — and holiness. However, unless we enter fully this dance of love, we might remain on the sidelines yearning for that which we already have.

The Sufis, who tap the essence of Islam as well as all religions, say: "Ishk Allah Ma'abud L'illah," that "God is Love, Lover and Beloved". There are magical moments when Joyce and I have overcome some great obstacle, and our eyes meet — and while I am seeing with the eyes of God the incredible perfection shining through Joyce, at the same time I feel God seeing me through Joyce's eyes, and together we are bathed in that luminous presence of love. Our relationship in those moments has become a vehicle for the Divine Being to see and be seen.

Thou wouldst not be searching for Me
If thou hadst not already found me.

PASCAL

PRACTICE

The following practice is our adaptation of a classical yoga exercise. Its purpose is to harmonize male and female energies inside us. When we bring these energies into balance, our relationships will also be balanced. The practice can be done alone or as a couple. It may seem complicated at first reading, but is really quite simple when put into practice.

Sit comfortably but with your spine straight. Close your eyes to minimize any visual interference.

Now using your right thumb, press your right nostril closed, and breathe in very slowly and very deeply. As you do this, feel a current of energy or sensation of any kind moving up the left side of your spine to the top of your head. At the same time know that this is your female nature, your receptivity, your feeling side, which you are now raising in consciousness, or waking up.

When you are finished breathing in ("inspiring"), also close your left nostril with your right index finger and pause a moment allowing your femaleness to be blessed by the Divine Mother, the female aspect of God.

Now release your thumb from your right nostril while still holding your left nostril closed. Slowly and deeply breathe out of the right nostril, while feeling a current of energy flow down the right side of your spine, reaching into the depth of your male nature.

Pause a moment after exhaling completely, then begin inhaling through the right nostril. As the current of energy ascends the right side of your spine, feel this as your male nature, your expressiveness, your thinking side. Allow all these aspects to ascend and be renewed. When the inhalation is complete, close both nostrils and again pause a moment while you allow your maleness to be blessed by the Heavenly Father, the male aspect of God.

Finally, open the left nostril and exhale, feeling the current of energy flow down the left side of your spine, delving once again into your femaleness.

Repeat this process and feel yourself come into balance, integrating your male and female energies into one harmonious whole.

three

The Way of Surrender

A friend is one to whom one may pour out all the contents of one's heart, chaff and grain together, knowing that the gentlest of hands will take and sift it, keep what is worth keeping, and with a breath of kindness blow the rest away.

ARABIAN PROVERB

Moses Mendelssohn, the grandfather of the well-known German composer, was far from being a handsome man. Along with a rather short stature, he also possessed a grotesque humpback.

Once, he visited a Hamburg merchant with a lovely daughter named Frumtje. Moses fell hopelessly in love with this young woman. But alas, Frumtje was repulsed by his misshapen appearance.

Finally, the time came for farewells. Moses gathered his courage and climbed the stairs to her room. She was a vision of heavenly beauty, but caused him deep sadness by her refusal to even look up at him. After several attempts at conversation, Moses shyly questioned, "Do you believe marriages are made in heaven?"

"Yes," she answered, still looking at the floor. "And do you?"

"Yes I do," he replied. "You see, in heaven at the birth of each boy, the Lord announces, 'This boy will marry that particular girl,' And when I was born, my future bride was pointed out to me, and then the Lord added, 'But your wife will be humpbacked.' "

"Right then and there I called out, 'Oh Lord, a humpbacked woman would be a tragedy. Please Lord, give me the hump and let her be beautiful.' "

Then Frumtje looked up into his eyes, and was stirred by some deep memory. She reached out and gave Mendelssohn her hand, and later became his devoted wife.

Mother Teresa of Calcutta consistently tells us true love is never possible without sacrifice, without surrender. Unless we give away that which is valuable to our ego, our little self, we cannot have the experience of real love. Ultimately, to experience perfect divine love, we must give away our very identity, that is, we must surrender our self-centered identification, the i that is not I.

A deep relationship is a training ground for learning surrender. This has not been an easy lesson for Joyce and me...

A man once called from Los Angeles, telling me he planned to marry his fiance in Santa Cruz in two months. He had somehow heard about us, and asked if we could marry them. The problem was, they wouldn't be able to meet us until a week before the wedding, when they planned to fly up. I had to decide via telephone, which I admit, was very hard for me. The couple seemed to be sincere. They wanted their wedding to reflect the merging and union they were experiencing. I told them it sounded good to me, but I had to sit with Joyce to feel what was best.

When I later told Joyce about this couple, a pained look came over her face. The more I tried to rationalize why we should do this wedding, the worse it got. I was doggedly explaining how a wedding is such a good opportunity to serve, and that maybe it's selfish to be so selective, when I finally noticed how heavy the energy between us had become. Something in me wanted to blame Joyce for this heaviness. Another part of me said, "Here we go again." I took a breath, held back my words, and asked inside what has happening. We were arguing, that's what! Here I had just told this man I needed to sit with Joyce to feel what was best, yet I was already attached to my own ideas.

How hard it is for me to let go of my ideas! Without exception, every idea or decision accompanied by that denseness between us has failed or proved wrong. When a decision is right, no matter how small or large, it is always accompanied by a feeling of lightness, joy, or ease, even if difficult to carry out.

Sometimes, when I'm mentally stuck on doing something, it sure seems like Joyce is standing in my way, and for a moment I'm a little boy rebelling against the restraints of my mother. Joyce may then momentarily doubt her feelings and accept this illusion. This is a way we become polarized (and paralyzed), two beings rather than one, and opposing each other.

In reality, Joyce has never stood in my way. I am the only one who can stand in my way, and I often do that through Joyce's being. In other words, when I became attached to my ideas about doing this particular wedding (which was actually not right for us to do), I was ignoring my heart, my intuition — the woman within me. Unconsciously then, I projected my inner woman onto Joyce and saw my hidden feelings expressed by her. This is the moment of truth, the moment of testing in every committed relationship. When I can surrender the supremacy of my thoughts over my feeling, when I open to my inner female, it is indeed a great victory.

One requirement of a spiritual friendship is learning to first listen within. We get ourselves into so much trouble by ignoring our inner guidance, the "still, small voice." When I ignore my guidance, it often will come through Joyce. It is as though God is trying to get all these messages through to me directly, and when I'm too preoccupied with my little desires, the messages must come through my environment. They might come through my daughters, the car, music, injuries, illnesses, anything. But very often they come through my wife. Because of our love, we become powerful instruments of change for each other.

The deeper the love of the couple, the more each becomes a mirror for the other. In the earlier days of our relationship, we seemed to get away with more. Subtle disharmonies, although unconscious and often passed over, would still have an effect on us. When we didn't hear the little promptings, more overt problems would result. Negative energy and feelings almost always start out small, and build until they are noticed. We need to see that this is nature's way of prompting us, because we have missed our internal cue. I think we all tend to be stubborn and preoccupied with ourselves. Add to this an unwillingness to admit it, and lots of problems arise.

The way of truth is the way of courage, and one of the most

courageous things I do in my life, and especially my marriage, is to admit my weaknesses. Can you see how this is not giving in to weaknesses? Most of us have such a strong defense of always being "right." In our divided way of being, we may feel rotten and insecure and defensive, yet outwardly we often present a picture of having it all together. We have set ourselves apart from God, from the wholeness of the universe, and so we are left scrambling to protect our measly portion. Until we again become one with all life, we will have anger, fear, sadness, doubt, and all kinds of negativity. Why guard all this? How freeing to admit it all, to surrender this defensiveness, and move on.

From what we have experienced, the love relationship between two beings accelerates this process of surrender. We love to watch this happen to newly-joined couples. Recently we watched a couple come together with great intensity. They were beautiful and inspiring to be around, for their egos had not yet entered strongly into the relationship. New lovers are a little like new babies. Their energy is truly heaven-like. Of course with babies there's the crying and fussing and sleepless nights, but the nearness to the higher worlds is remarkable, and the power definite, if you're *still* enough to experience it. And it may continue for months. Likewise, in a new relationship there may also be crying and fussing and sleepless nights. In the same way the heavens are opened, for love has just been reborn in the hearts of the lovers, and personality features are put on "hold." It, too, may continue for months.

Inevitably, however, the infant is redressed in the cloak of personality, reassuming its karmic work on earth, and that ineffable radiance seems to dim somewhat. Lost? No. It is just temporarily hidden until reawakened consciously later on, when it will be stronger as a result of overcoming.

So too with this couple, the temporary displacement of ego-natures caused them to marvel at their oneness. Arguing was simply an impossibility, so magical was their respect for each other. We watched them walking, arm-in-arm, that new-born lover's mist filling their eyes. For a moment, we wished we could protect them in some way from the harshness of the ego-cloaking, in the same way we felt with both of our daughters.

We saw this same woman sometime later. She looked much more grounded, yet a little sad. We asked how things were going. With a hint of a smile that revealed at least some understanding of the whole process, she admitted that they were arguing more and more over smaller and smaller details of their life. She had been so sure they would never have problems!

The taste of unconditional love will often do this. It creates the illusion of permanence. Really, it is permanent, for pure love is the most solid thing there is. The problem has to do with lack of surrender. All of us at some time in our lives are shown "the heavenly vision", whether it's by loving another, or through some spiritual method, or in a spontaneous receptive moment. But we lack complete surrender to this, the highest truth we have experienced. In other words, we still think we have other things to do or be.

Can you remember being so in love that nothing else mattered at all? Or that the world was standing still, and only you and your beloved existed? Yet in the next moment some totally trivial thought enters your mind, and you've lost the feeling...seemingly forever. Maybe you feel like some cosmic joke's been played on you, or even that you've been punished.

Not at all! It's just that you've touched upon the center of life, a deeper, more essential reality. But you've lacked the strength and preparedness to sustain this consciousness. You've lacked the discipline and one-pointedness of mind to stay focused. Yet the experience has become a part of you, has whetted your appetite for more. A taste of such loveliness will pull on your heart for all time, not letting you rest until by conscious effort you've regained this "lost paradise."

The Parsival myth depicts this wonderfully. Early in his journey, Parsival is permitted entry into the grail castle (heaven) where his consciousness is raised to ecstasy, which is the Christ-Consciousness. He lacks a deep enough surrender to his ideal, and this brings him down. He then spends the remainder of the legend gaining mastery over himself, living through desire after desire, constantly driven by the remembrance of how it was — and is! Finally, when he surrenders all his desires to the one desire for the Holy Grail, to God, he regains heavenly consciousness.

It was necessary for this couple friend of ours to go through the same process. Falling in love, or better, rising in love, opens the doors to the heaven experience, which most can only sustain for a short time. One by one, the lesser desires of this man and woman brought them both down. These human desires reflect the habits, roles, self-images, and expectations which must be cleared before surrender can take place — not surrender to each other, *but surrender to love.*

The purity and power of real love shines light on the flaws and weaknesses of personality. This is part of the test of Divine Love.

The couple, by touching upon Divine Love, sees also each other's faults, or rather, sees their own faults projected upon each other. It is love which is doing this, but because they don't see this, they start fighting and bickering.

True surrender takes so much courage! It is admitting to the negativity within us, rather than projecting it onto our mate, blaming him or her. True surrender involves honoring the natural process of unfolding, remembering that the light of love is illuminating the dark places within us, opening our closet doors one by one and gently irradiating their contents. The process of true surrender can be quite painful, but the surrender itself is exhilirating and joyous, not painful. *The pain is due to our clinging to who we think we are, and what we think should be happening.*

Every relationship of love is like the relationship between the master and disciple, with each person in the couple containing the essence of both the master and the disciple. The master reflects with mirror-accuracy every thought and feeling of the disciple. It is the love and stillness of the master which alone can do this. As long as the disciple holds onto anything less than love, suffering is the result.

The spiritual marriage is the same thing, only we often fail to realize that it is the master with whom we are relating and who is also relating through us. We often fail to realize that we will only be happy when we surrender to the will of the master...which is identical to the will of God within us.

Our partner will so often reflect, as the master does, what we are thinking and feeling, how we are hiding from ourselves, and to what foolishness we are clinging. The more love felt, the more in tune the couple is, the more intense this mirroring will be.

This is one of the hardest lessons couples have to learn. So many separations happen because one or both partners are not willing to surrender to the intensity of this reflective process. They forget or do not see the master who is testing them. They hold on to the testing part, the heaviness of the relationship, and the feeling so easily becomes, ''I don't have to put up with this anymore. I can be free just by leaving...''

It is possible, however, to remember that the hand of the master has caused these tests, not to punish us, but to give us the extraordinary opportunity to become masters ourselves. It is very possible to see the eyes of the master looking at us through the eyes of our partner, perhaps even twinkling a bit, revealing the kind of love that longs to see us let go of our pain. It is also very

possible to feel the presence of the Living Spirit overshadowing and interpenetrating our own being, and feel our negativity dissolve like mists under the radiant morning sun.

four

Trial By Fire

To enter the valley of love, one must plunge wholly into fire. Yes, one must become fire itself, for otherwise one cannot live there. He that truly loves must resemble fire, his countenance aflame, burning and impetuous like fire.

FARID UD-DIN ATTAR

It was a glorious, cool and colorful early November day. We were on a camping trip to our favorite place: Mt. Shasta, California. Some friends were watching four-year-old Rami for a night and a day, a very rare treat...it gave us time to be just Barry and me. We were both just as happy as could be as we hiked the slopes of Mt. Shasta, stopping to kiss and feel how very much we loved each other.

We decided to go to Panther Meadows at 7500 feet. It was gorgeous, with scattered patches of snow, a little stream bubbling icy water, the glistening white mountain towering above us. The

air seemed charged with electricity and I felt as though I could fly.
Instead I danced throughout the meadow. Barry laughed and
caught me in his arms. There was so much love our bodies begged
to be closer, so we retreated to our little VW Camper, where we
merged physically, emotionally and spiritually. During the height
of this experience we both simultaneously felt the nearness of a
third being, a great and majestic Presence. It seemed like this
presence, whom we could not see, was pouring forth love and
blessing us.

Back in our home three days later in Santa Cruz I was lying
down to take a short nap. Something within me felt different. As I
felt my body I realized intuitively that an egg and sperm had joined
in union. I was pregnant. Tears of gratitude filled me and I rose to
pray and give thanks. For the next ten days I felt a beautiful soul so
close to me that I could almost reach out and touch this being of
light. With each new day I grew to love this being more and more. I
was so thrilled that this soul was coming to us. My hopes and
dreams took off like a sky rocket. I felt so much in love.

Soon after, Barry took Rami for a little overnight camping trip.
I was so happy to be alone — to love and dream of my new baby.

Then suddenly I began to bleed and bleed. My baby was leaving me and I ached so much. Why couldn't I keep you? Did you find me unworthy to be your mother? I miss you so much.

I had heard of the loneliness and despair that women experience when they lose a baby through miscarriage. I never really understood it until it happened to me. It was as though a great treasure were suddenly pulled away from me, even after only ten days. When I was finally able to still the storm of emotion enough, I asked inside, "Why couldn't I carry my baby, Lord? Is there something wrong with me?" And the answer so lovingly reassured me that this child would come to us, but we were not yet ready. There would be certain tests and preparations to ready us. We should be thankful when the tests come as well as remembering why they come.

One week later my most beloved friend in the animal kingdom died quite suddenly. Bokie was our ten-year-old Golden Retriever. How deeply I adored that boy! He wasn't a dog to me. He was my friend, my first child, a comforter, my teacher and a mother. Whenever I felt really sad and could not be with Barry or Rami, I'd turn to Bo and put my arms around his body. He had so much compassion in him, as if he could take the pain away. It seemed his

greatest pleasure came from just being near us and pouring forth love from his huge liquid brown eyes. His health seemed to suddenly fail right after the miscarriage, and he grew worse and worse and died within a week. What a hard test! I had never before felt the pangs of death so deeply. We were thrown into a new experience: grieving. It was like he sacrificed himself for our sake. It took me a long time to stop missing his lovable body and begin to feel his essence — to know that he would always be with us.

Test after test followed, and at times I felt lost under the burden of it all, forgetting that there was any meaning. At one point Barry felt a pain in his kidney area. Over the days the pain grew worse and worse. As other mysterious symptoms developed, he pulled his medical books off the shelf and read and read and felt worse and worse. It did not look very good. He was deciding to submit himself to a whole series of tests at the hospital where he worked. As a doctor and nurse we are trained to suspect the worst. In my corner, I was terrified! Despite my efforts to push it away, I felt an immanence...or an aura...of death. What if Barry died? Could I go on without him? As his pain grew worse, my fears crowded in more and more, haunting me day and night.

Finally we each went off by ourselves and confronted our fears. I felt how much I loved Barry. I felt the qualities in him that I loved the most, and I again began to feel Barry's essence. I realized he would be with me always — as strongly in death as in life. Our bodies may die, but our loving will only grow. Our uniting will always continue. I felt ready to accept whatever was to come. Barry similarly had an experience of accepting death and feeling our eternal unity. It had been a hard struggle for us both to arrive at just one moment of perceiving truth. But that one moment of truth, though not always present, is stored permanently in our consciousness. We came together and held each other a long, long time. We felt such thankfulness to be able to share our journeys together and ready for whatever God had in store for us. After that day, the pain and symptoms Barry was feeling gradually faded until there were none.

Then Christmas night I sat alone listening to special Christmas music. Christmas with Barry and Rami had been very meaningful this year. We had concentrated on the word "Emmanuel," how God dwells within us. On the radio came a newly written song using the word "Emmanuel." I felt a warm glow and opening sensation in my heart. Then I felt another presence beside me and I heard these gentle words within me:

"You are now ready. I am coming as your friend to help bring you closer to God."

Tears of joy filled my being. Emmanuel, God within man, was felt within me. Another manifestation of God's love was coming to us.

We had allowed ourselves to become buried under the tests. Only rarely had we climbed the mountain of consciousness to see an overview, to see a divine purpose and intention behind all that was happening to us. Gradually, we remembered our experience on Mt. Shasta, conceiving and then losing our child, with the promise of its return after our testing and preparation. Then we realized how all the tests were bringing us to the point of readiness for this new blessing in our lives. A strong inner prompting set us out once again toward Mt. Shasta, where we again conceived our second child and at the same time conceived the vision of this book.

The tests come. They must. Our earth experience is like a school where we learn and must be tested by our teachers. Just as in school where we must study and pass an exam before we can go on, so it is in life. We must learn and then be tested by the teacher within us — our real self. When we pass — and this may take years — new growth, new freedom and understanding, a new blessing awaits us.

As couples, we long to merge into oneness, to feel Divine Love continuously. We may get a taste of what it is like, but then we must prove our readiness before we are allowed to dwell in that space for long. The secret is to stay aware of the divine intention behind the tests, and feel grateful and blessed when they come.

five

Commitment and Marriage

For even as love crowns you so shall he crucify you. Even as he is for your growth so is he for your pruning.

Even as he ascends to your height and caresses your tenderest branches that quiver in the sun,

So shall he descend to your roots and shake them in their clinging to the earth.

KAHLIL GIBRAN

One day Barry and I went to our local produce market with our daughter, Rami. While we were happily picking out some delicious summer berries, we overheard a middle-aged woman discussing marriage with the younger male checker. The man, who happened to be a friend of ours, had been with his wife for over fifteen years.

The woman was quite upset about something and loudly declared to the man, "Your generation knows so little about real marriage!" She then went on to relate how she had been late in purchasing a wedding present for her favorite niece. There had been a big wedding, and yet for some reason it had taken the woman four months to deliver her expensive, and thoughtfully-picked present. The niece had gratefully accepted the present, but then told her aunt that she and her husband had since separated and were filing for a divorce. The woman said this was the second time this had happened to her. It seemed she couldn't buy a present quick enough before the couple were divorced. She then looked at the three of us and said, "What is the matter with today's young couples? Don't they realize marriage is an up and down situation?" We all quietly smiled and shrugged off the question, but I pondered it a great deal throughout the day, as I had also known of many similar situations. The shortest marriage I was aware of lasted three weeks.

Through our counseling work Barry and I are sometimes asked to perform a wedding ceremony. This is a serious, special, and sacred act for us, and we question the couple very deeply before the wedding takes place. We are not interested in performing a wedding because the couple thinks marriage would be fun, or convenient, or worth a try. We are only interested when the couple wants to enter into a spiritual marriage. A question that we always ask is, "Are you willing to commit yourselves to each other and to the process of merging spiritually for a lifetime?" For those who are committed, an answer of "yes" comes very easily. Of course, things come up and perhaps a marriage commitment need be broken. However, to answer "yes" to that question is to sense the meaning behind the words — to feel the intention within your heart.

A while ago I was visiting with a friend. She was very excited because her former husband was traveling 3,000 miles to see her for her birthday. At first I thought that was very strange. They never had children together and she had been happily married to a wonderful man for eight years — and they had three small children. I questioned her as to why she even wanted this other man to visit.

Her reply was so beautiful: "Ten years ago we committed ourselves to loving each other until death. Every two years or so we renew our friendship and love, the same way a brother and sister would do."

She went on to explain that in their second year of marriage they realized they were not meant to be married to each other. Knowing they were needing to go in different directions, they decided they didn't want to end the relationship in anger or hatred, but instead with deep understanding. Before they permanently separated they had a little ceremony between them, during which they went over their marriage vows and committed themselves instead to a life-long friendship. Whether they saw each other or not, they agreed to always think of the positive qualities of each other — to remember each other in love. The marriage had ended, but the commitment of friendship had started to blossom.

Ending her first marriage in such a clear and conscious way freed this woman to enter into a very deep and long-lasting relationship with her present husband. It is anger, hate, jealousy or resentment toward a former partner that prevents a person from fully committing themselves to a new partner. The only way to close the door permanently on one marriage and open to a new commitment is to close the door with love, forgiveness and understanding. Negative feelings, however buried, are like a foot in the door of an old relationship. No matter how hard the door is pushed it can never fully close. Until it fully closes, the new door of commitment and love can never fully open.

For those who really aren't sure in their hearts that marriage is right for them, a thousand excuses fly through the air as to why they could never answer "yes" to a lifetime commitment. Perhaps then it is best to wait to marry. During a period of six years we performed only seven marriages, and all seven couples were ready for that type of commitment. We have seen these couples go through extreme ups and downs and yet, because of the commitment, their love continues to grow increasingly toward the place of oneness.

Since our wedding in 1968, Barry and I have experienced many ups and downs. Many times one of us has felt inside, "It isn't worth it anymore. I just want to give up and live alone." And yet in the lowest times, when I was almost ready to pack my bags, that lovely inner voice would ask me to surrender, to forgive, to see my own mistakes rather than Barry's, and to give up just a little more of my own self-righteousness. I would be asked to merge and grow, rather than take the easy way out and give up. Barry and I would then come together and give up a little more of our clinging to our egos, and find ourselves merged a little more deeply. After these experiences the love would always be stronger, and deeper, and filled with more respect and understanding — both for each other and for ourselves. We had climbed another step on the ladder, had passed one of the many tests required of couples who are seeking that fathomless love of true union.

If you desire a spiritual marriage you must give up desiring a life of ease and contentment that never rocks the boat. Instead, you are both wanting to burn together. You are wanting to invite the spiritual fires of purification into your lives, after which you stand not as two separate beings, but as One — united with each other and with all of humanity. Your marriage has in this way been a school room, where you have learned the rules of life: giving, loving, surrendering, and being thankful. Your marriage has been the process of pruning, after which you finally emerge as masters of yourselves. In learning to live in perfect harmony with one other person, you have learned to live in harmony with the world. It is sometimes a hard road, but the rewards are so wonderful that we feel fully dedicated to this process in our own lives as well as other couples wanting to take this step.

Once, Barry and I were invited to the wedding of a very dedicated and committed couple. It was obvious to us and to all who met them that their love for each other was very deep and sustaining. In fact, it was a great privilege to be at their wedding, for the power of love was so strongly felt.

For the next two and one-half years we saw them off and on. They went through ups and downs, but always their love grew. People would tell us that just to be near this couple would make them happy, their love was so infectious. One day we received a call from the couple. The man got on the phone first and said, "I've done something so terrible, I don't think I'll ever be worthy of my wife's love again." The woman then got on the phone and, through much crying, was able to communicate that they'd reached the lowest point in their marriage. She wanted to go on but didn't know if she could. We set up a meeting with them as soon as we could.

When they arrived at our door for the appointed meeting, they were indeed a downcast-looking two-some. The man came in with head lowered and would not look us in the eyes. The woman burst into tears and could hardly stop crying. Barry and I sat down quietly in anticipation of the story to come. Having experienced many low periods ourselves, we were convinced that nothing was so bad that love could not heal it. The man began his sad tale of how he had come home late from work feeling very off-center from the events of the day. While he was driving home he pictured his wife, all loving and warm, and imagined she would help him to feel centered and happy again. When he entered the house, however, he found his wife in a similar state, having also had a hard day at work. She had been waiting for him, hoping he could lift her spirits!

This is such a typical scenario. They were both disappointed, of course, and soon started arguing. He suggested that they both be alone, and he stomped off to the bedroom. She followed him and started accusing him of not caring, etc. In the next instant his hand flew out and hit her in the mouth, which instantly began to bleed. They were both shocked, as he had never hit her before. He left the house horrified by his own behavior, and was convinced he was unworthy of ever receiving love again. He was so upset that he drove to an orchard and lay down under a tree for the night. A policeman found him at four in the morning and, after hearing his tale, suggested he go see a psychologist at the county mental health department. He made an emergency appointment for the next morning and the psychologist (probably in fear of his own aggressive nature) confirmed our friend's belief that he indeed had a grave problem. He left the psychologist's office feeling even worse. The next week was apparently very hard for the couple. The man was so convinced he was unlovable that he filled his mind with thoughts of self-blame and punishment. Behind his wall of self-condemnation, he was unable to reach out and give love. His wife sat in loneliness and despair, and tried to make up stories for others to explain her swollen, purple lip.

Having completed their story, the couple stared at the floor. Barry and I looked at each other and smiled as memories of our periods of despair came flooding to the surface. We felt so much love for each other in that moment, for we sensed very deeply that without those periods of despair we would not have turned so deeply to God for help, and our love now would not be so beautiful. I then shared with the couple a similar experience in which I felt I could never forgive Barry again for something he had done. He had similarly enclosed himself in a wall of self-punishment, feeling he could never forgive himself.

This situation continued for several days. On the fourth day I picked up one of my favorite spiritual books and held it close to my heart. I prayed and prayed and, with all the sincerity of my being, I asked for help. I then trusted fully that God would guide me through words in this book. I closed my eyes and opened the book.

My eyes fell upon a Biblical quote, "Bear ye one another's burdens." The author then went on to explain that true brotherhood will not come to earth until we are willing to share each other's weaknesses and burdens, and climb towards God together. I felt inside how I could no longer go on seeing a certain situation as just Barry's big problem. I had to accept my responsibility in the situation and learn ways I was contributing to it. If we continued as we had, seeing each other as having a big individual problem and disliking that in the other, then we would continue to pull each other down. I then realized that as we shared each problem together, we would rise together.

Tears of joy and gratitude filled me. God had helped and my heart had opened to Barry for the first time in four days. I wanted to once again share his weaknesses, and for him to share mine...to be as One growing together rather than two pushing each other down. The healing power of love can cure even the worst weakness within us. I pictured Barry in that moment and he was so beautiful. Yes, there were weaknesses and flaws within him, yet they were so small compared to his greatness. I saw how I could either magnify the beauty, the God-self in him, or the small part that remained unconscious. I could help him feel more of his beauty, or help him feel more of his weakness. We have such creative power in each other's lives! By loving and accepting the weakness — in me as well as him — a healing could take place, and those weaker areas could be turned to strengths. What a powerful moment for me! It was a turning point in my life — and in our marriage. I was able to go to Barry with so much love that it helped him to also feel the inspiration. Ever since then we have tried to work together on problems, rather than blaming and pushing each other down. Of course, we've slipped in this process many times, but it has helped me tremendously to try and magnify the God in each other and pour healing love on the yet unconscious parts. God asks only that we try, pick ourselves up when we've fallen, and try again.

There was silence in the room when I finished my little story. The woman looked at her husband and tears of love flowed from her eyes. She told him how much she loved him, and soon they were embracing. She also told him how much she had contributed to his hitting her by pushing him into a corner, and that she knew she must take half of the blame upon herself. His heart opened then and he allowed love to come in. He saw that it wasn't he alone that had this insurmountable problem. Now they *shared* a problem and through love and communication could conquer it. Most importantly, they both realized they could not expect that centered feeling to come from the other, but must first make the effort to find it within themselves. It would take work and patience on both of their parts the next time a similar situation occurred, but they both realized their love and commitment could heal this and all wounds, bringing them strength and deeper love.

Barry and I looked at each other as the couple embraced once more. In that moment I experienced a great depth of love for Barry and gratitude for all the hard times we've had to experience. For those of you who have gone through a dark period with your loved one and then finally come out into the light, you know of the love of which I speak. It is a love that says "I know your worst side now and still I love you more than ever. I love you totally now, your beauty, your strengths, your weaknesses, your all." Then you look into the eyes of your beloved, and it is like looking into the eyes of God, the All-Seeing One. To be loved and to love so fully is one of the most wonderful experiences life has to offer.

It is easy to love a person because they are wonderful, but the whole test of love is to love a person despite the fact that they do not live up to what one sees in them.

PIR VILAYAT INAYAT KHAN

You should love everyone as God and love each other. If you cannot love each other you cannot achieve your goal.

NEEM KAROLI BABA (MAHARAJJI)

Let a man overcome anger by love; let him overcome evil by good; let him overcome the greedy by generosity, and a liar by the truth. For hatred does not cease by hatred at anytime; hatred ceases by love...

GAUTAMA BUDDHA

When you observe imperfection in another individual, if you will hold your thought to perfection and release your love and your own power of perfection into the world of the other, you will render a service you little dream possible.

SAINT GERMAIN

The Wedding Ceremony

If I can remember who I AM,
I will always know who loves me.
  All of nature sings this song,
  And if I listen closely
  I know who loves me.
Would you care to share the climb with me,
Find the air so clear and rare?
We can see so far from there,
Crescent moon and star from there.
  And the wings of our hearts
  Lift us peacefully
  As we sail into the sun.
If I can remember who I AM,
I will always know who loves me.

MARK'S SONG TO NANCY,
WRITTEN THE NIGHT BEFORE THEIR WEDDING.

When two or more are gathered in My name,
there I AM...

MATTHEW 18:20

We are occasionally called upon to marry couples, especially those we have worked deeply with in counseling. With these couples the wedding ceremony becomes the culmination of all we have experienced together. A wedding is a couple's proclamation of commitment; not only to each other but to the spiritual path ahead. Marriage is joining hands and hearts together for greater service to God and humanity. True, a committed couple can do this without being married. But to do this among friends and family, in the highly focused energy and power of a spiritual ceremony, makes a permanent imprint of all that takes place, and greatly benefits the couple. Many people are not aware that angels and a whole host of invisible beings are drawn together by any gathering with a sincere, heart-felt motive. It is their work to help redirect all the energies and thought-forms released by the participants. Ordinary thoughts or negative energies are ignored, in the same way that bees ignore all but the flower's ripe pollen. In a wedding these unseen beings help to gather and focus the love of everyone present onto the couple, providing a sustaining strength for their relationship.

The wedding can set the tone of the couple's entire life together, for the wedding ceremony is the visible symbol of the ongoing wedding process in which two beings grow in union. It is also the symbol of the "mystical marriage," which is the inner wedding — the merging of the male with the female elements within each person. This inner wedding puts an end to projection, anger, or hurt because you see in your husband or wife not only a part of yourself, but also the loveliness of creation. Your love for all of creation becomes an expression of your love for your own being as a child of God.

Learning to love one other person completely teaches you how to love all people. Learning to love all that is unlovable in your husband or wife, learning how to rise above the pettiness, disagreements, judgments, and human preoccupations, establishes in you a love for all humanity. For if you are a committed couple, every grievance you have with life, with God, every trait you dislike in yourself, you will sooner or later project onto your partner. The closer you become to another human being, the more this person will mirror those qualities in yourself that you are not at peace with. If your are courageous, marriage and the committed love relationship will provide deep personal growth.

The wedding ceremony is sacred and is not to be taken lightly. Rather, it is one of the heavenly initations enacted on earth which couples must pass through joyfully on their journey to Oneness. The right spirit of love and dedication will provide a sustaining force throughout their lives.

Choosing the right person or persons to marry you is very important if you want the wedding to reflect something of its heavenly purpose. Choose someone who believes in marriage and believes in your love together as a couple.

When we went to get our wedding license in 1968, we had to go to a small county office. There was a policy in that office that all who came for a wedding license had to visit the Justice of the Peace. This man had the legal right to marry people, and performed many ceremonies in his office. We entered his office to find a big, middle-aged man. He shook our hands and with a doubtful look gave us a little wooden shamrock. "What is this for?" we asked. "It's for good luck in your marriage," he replied. "You'll need it. Marriages always fail these days. I thought I'd try giving out good luck charms." Imagine how hard it would be to start your marriage with such doubt from the person marrying you?

When we were planning for our wedding, it was very difficult to find someone to marry us. It was uncommon in those days for a Jewish/Christian wedding to take place. It was assumed one of us would change for the other. We very much wanted a spiritual wedding service and wondered who would perform such a wedding. People on both sides of our families questioned the rightness of our union. No one from either the church or the temple seemed ready to take the risk. One leader told us we had no right to marry. Finally we found a man who was different. He cared little about our backgrounds. He wanted to know if we really loved each other. After talking with us for a while, he looked at us both long and hard. Then his eyes softened and he said, "You do love each other very much. I will be happy to help you marry." In that moment a connection was established. He had looked into our lives and believed in our love and eternal union.

The belief the person marrying you has in your togetherness is extremely important as well as sustaining. This person must also have a belief in marriage as a uniting process. If not, he or she will be an impure channel and your initiation may be affected in some way. This does not mean that you need a "guru" or high spiritual leader to perform the wedding. Your Great Uncle from his little country church would be just perfect if in his heart he believed in marriage.

It is also essential that this person take the time to look into your lives to feel within himself or herself the rightness of your union and be able to bless it fully. With a belief in marriage and a belief in your union together, this person can be used as a powerful channel for God's love. His or her hand upon you at the close of the ceremony, free from doubt or pessimism, will be used by God to transmit a blessing upon your lives. In other words, there has to be a spiritual connection between the couple and those conducting the ceremony. When you meet with that person or persons, trust that you will feel the rightness in your heart.

The wedding ceremony is a creative act and is unique to each couple. No two weddings are alike, just as no two couples are alike. You won't find your wedding in a wedding manual, with blank spaces where you fill in your names. There is no work involved in that type of wedding. A truly powerful and inspiring wedding ceremony takes a lot of joyful work and creativity which is symbolic of what it takes to make a relationship be continously growing and loving. The main emphasis for the wedding day should be to make the ceremony as deeply moving an experience for everyone present as possible. To merely recite lines from a book, to say "I do" and get the ceremony over as quickly as possible to move on to the party, is also symbolic of how much a couple will really work afterwards to make their marriage truly divine.

Depending on the spiritual path the couple is following, they can adopt the ceremony of that religion and add their own creative touches in the appropriate places. One particular ceremony we attended for example was a formal Hindu ceremony in which the couple changed the traditional Hindu vows into vows that were relevant and appropriate for their relationship, making the ceremony very meaningful for them.

Every wedding needs coherence and tradition. It must emerge from an archetypal ceremony, a heavenly wedding blueprint, designed to give power and strength to your union. A "true" wedding will be your unique expression of this pattern, and being in love will allow you both to see and understand its manifestation in your lives. We have outlined a universal ceremony that we use. We hope it sparks ideas that a couple might use to create their own wedding.

As with all ceremonies, there are three main parts: a beginning, a body, and a closing. The first part is the invocation. This is the call to God, the Universal Spirit and Power. The sincerity of the invocation sets the tone of the entire wedding, and determines whether it will be heaven-made or human-made. This is the time to focus the energy and unite all those present. It is the time to help still people's minds and bring them into their hearts, to momentarily leave their daily lives and enter the temple of love. Spoken prayers, meditations, music and singing all help.

To begin the second part, or body of the wedding, we ask the couple to include their parents or parent in the ceremony. Again this is up to the couple's creativity. We feel it is very important to remember and be grateful to the dear people we call our parents, who have guided and helped us to come to this point in our journey. Pouring as much love out to them as possible, your gratitude is a very beautiful way of saying good-bye to one relationship you've had with them, as well as greeting the new one to come. In each wedding we've taken part in, this exchange has been deeply moving and inspirational for all. Many simply thank their parents for all they've been given. However it is done, the flow of love going from child to parent and back again helps strengthen the couple in their love for each other.

Next, before the couple says their vows to one another, we direct all those present to close their eyes. We ask them to remember the important vows they have made in this life, such as wedding vows, vows to serve, vows to love their children. Then we ask them to go deeper still and try to remember the vow they made before coming to earth: the vow to use this life to come into greater light and to love one another as deeply as possible. Such a remembrance seems difficult for people in their everyday consciousness. However, during the magic of the wedding ceremony all are uplifted, and while their attention is drawn to this very important vow, they can sometimes re-experience it and once again find the strength of it within themselves.

We feel that the vows and any symbolic gestures, such as rings or whatever, should come from the inspiration of the couple. How each couple proclaims their commitment to each other and to God is their special gift and offering to the world. A certain couple immediately comes to mind. When they asked us to marry them, they meant just that! Both of them being somewhat inward and shy, they announced their intentions to remain silent for the entire ceremony. We said no. We would only help with the wedding. If nothing else, they would have to create and say their vows to each other. Otherwise they would have to find someone else. They left visibly upset, and for some time struggled with their decision. They even called on the phone to plead with us to let them remain silent. "No," we again said. More time went by. Finally they decided to do it, admitting great fear.

They wrote poems to each other from the deepest feelings in their hearts. During the wedding, when the time came for their vows, we had them turn and face each other. The silence was penetrating. The woman unfolded her piece of paper, looked at it, and with a choked-up voice got out one line before her voice quit totally. A tear slid down her cheek as she tried again, but to no avail, while her husband-to-be looked on in bewilderment and an awkward hush fell upon all present. Then with a burst of energy, she started crying and pouring out her feelings in words. She embraced her beloved, who in tears also, started expressing his feelings. And do you know, everyone there started crying and holding each other! At that moment, the wedding had happened, for all of us had become united into one being.

It didn't matter whether they said their vows or not. All that mattered was their intention. Had they remained silent as they wished, this merging might not have happened. For a wedding is also an initiation, a facing of oneself. There has to be some kind of overcoming of fear or embarrassment. If the couple remains comfortable and secure, the depth of feeling required may not be reached.

Along with the vows, the wedding archetype includes the use of symbols. An exchange of rings is deeply imbedded in many traditions. The ring is the circle, the symbol of the world, with no beginning or end. It is the symbol of the cycles of life. Exchanging rings denotes commitment to life, to fulfilling the plan of nature, and fulfilling your purpose on earth. The ring encloses your finger the same way that your earthly commitments enclose your life, until you fulfill your destiny of perfect love and service to God and humanity.

At our own wedding in 1968, we decided to incorporate a little candlelighting ceremony. One main candle on the altar symbolized the Light of God. From this Eternal Light we each kindled our individual candles, drawing our heart's love from the One Source. Then, holding our lit candles in one hand, and joining our other hands, we said our vows to each other.

For a couple to create their own ritual, indeed, to create the whole wedding ceremony, it involves a high level of cooperation and compromise (compromising = promising together). This process of working together to shape their wedding can be very meaningful to the couple, for it is also shaping the visions and dreams of their lives and work together. It is a merging of two individual's creative abilities, and unlike mathematical theory, this merged creativity is far greater than the sum of the two parts.

Finally we come to the third part of the wedding ceremony — the closing. This is the benediction or blessing — putting into God's hands all that the couple has done together and, especially, all that they will do. The wedding officiants say a prayer of blessing, and proclaim the marriage.

At this point we always include all those present and ask everyone to bless the couple, send them love, or pray for them. At a recent wedding we asked everyone to come forward. (The ceremony was held in a state park amphitheater under the redwoods. The hundred or so people seemed too spread out on the bench-like seats.) With the two of us and the couple forming the center of a very densely-packed group, we asked everyone first to silently bless the couple, to unite all our energies with the purpose of helping them in their life ahead. Then we taught everyone a simple, but very beautiful, blessing song:

May the blessings of God rest upon you.
May God's peace abide with you.
May God's presence illuminate your hearts
Now and forevermore.

Everyone sang this blessing to the couple and, while doing so, we had everyone hold their hands up, palms facing the couple, pouring out the blessings of God through their hands. This was a deeply moving experience for all of us. One older woman was so touched, she later told us she had never experienced such a flow of God's love through her own being.

Lastly, it is our deepest heart-felt feeling that the wedding ceremony is an act of service. Far more than anything that happens to the couple, the wedding to us is a way to bring more light into the world, to help raise the consciousness of humanity. The couples who have shared this feeling with us have experienced a deep merging during their weddings. The scope of the wedding is widened from the individual to the global perspective. A ceremony of this nature is an opportunity to help open the hearts of all who attend. The sweetness and openness of newlyweds is infectious and touches all who are present. While attending a friend's wedding in 1965, our eyes were opened to the vision of our love and, in tears of joy, we knew someday we would also be getting married.

Robin and Saladin's Wedding Vows • May 7, 1978

Saladin: *May we remain as ideals in each other's eyes so that*
by concentrating on all that is good in each other we will come to
embody those ideals.

Robin: *May we not dwell upon each other's faults, but rather*
rise together on wings of acceptance and recognize the divinity
within each.

Saladin: *Let us be ever mindful of the Divine Sculptor*
working through us who, in time, will shape us revealing our
true nature.

Robin: *May we remain awake in times of adversity and make*
use of these times as a means for growth and realization.

Saladin: *May this special relationship based on love and*
acceptance serve as a model for our relationship with the world in
general.

Robin: *May our understanding of love deepen through our*
years together and may that love be an offering of service to life.

seven

Like Potter's Clay

What your attention is upon, you become.

PEARL DORRIS

Love's creative power is awesome! Through deep love and surrender we can be like clay molded by the hands of our beloved into perfection. By focusing on the beauty and greatness in one another, we can actually bring it to the surface. We each have a tremendous responsibility to those we love, especially those closest to us. The more beauty we can see in others the more beauty we can see in ourselves. As we hold fast to the beauty in others, so do we also become beautiful.

On the contrary, when we see the negative in others, especially our mates, so do we also become negative. Our beloved is a part of our own being, and as we see him or her, so do we see ourselves. To pick out a part of our beloved and say, ''I don't like that,'' is like cutting out a part of one's own being, closing a vital door leading to the heart. We need our hearts to be open so we may fully receive God's light and love. Seeing the inner beauty and greatness in others is a powerful and creative way to keep our hearts open.

While Barry and I lived in Los Angeles, I had a wonderful spiritual teacher who happened to come in the package of a twenty-two year old woman. As soon as I saw her I knew she had a great amount to teach me. She practiced a very unusual hobby, one that I needed and wanted desperately to learn. She looked for and saw beauty in others. This was her fun and joy — her life. I had never met anyone like that before.

I asked this woman to teach me her hobby. She agreed and started by taking me to the Los Angeles Airport. I groaned inside as we drove to the airport. I hated crowds of people. She sat me right down in the busiest section. At first I felt overwhelmed by the noise and confusion. Then she started pointing out beauty in the people who hurried by:

"Look at that woman, and how deeply she loves her baby. Look at that man over there. Can you see how his eyes are twinkling as he carries that specially wrapped package? He must be such a giving person. Oh, look at that great smile on that old woman. How much joy she has! And look at that man who seems to appear so serious. Can you see how deeply sensitive he is to life?"

This went on for an hour and I began to feel lighter and lighter. By the time we left I could have floated home. The crowd was no longer noisy and confusing, nor a threat to my peace of mind. It had become one vast moving being of great loveliness. By focusing on so much beauty in others, we had touched all those places in ourselves and started to soar in the process. My friend didn't know or intellectually understand this. To her it had always simply been a lot of fun.

Most people are conditioned to observe others in only superficial ways. For example, some middle-aged friends of ours are somewhat overweight. They are so conscious of being overweight that they always see people through that filter: "I saw Connie yesterday. She's gained." "How's Bill doing? Did he lose?" "Martha always eats too much!" With each statement they make about a person's weight, it only reinforces their own feelings about being overweight.

At first it takes a little concentration to train yourself to see beauty and strength beneath the surface appearance. But every effort will be greatly rewarded, as the following story illustrates:

When our first daughter, Rami, was four years old, she and I had a special experience while walking on the beach. We saw a man in his sixties collecting soda cans and placing them into a big bag. He appeared to be extremely sad, so much so that his whole body bent under the weight of it. I might not have noticed him, except that Rami pointed him out saying, "Mama, why is that man so sad? He looks like he could cry any minute." I really had to agree with her. Then I told her that we could help. I suggested to her that we send him love and joy, and try to see him as happy. We passed him several times, and each time we passed we would imagine him as happy. An hour went by in which we didn't see him, so we thought he probably went home. As we were climbing the long series of steps to our car we heard someone running up after us. We turned around and there was the same man. He had a broad smile on his face and awkwardly remarked to us, "Gee it's a nice day isn't it?"

That experience reaffirmed for me the power of concentrating on the positive. It was amazing to witness such a drastic change in a complete stranger. Now can you just imagine the power and change possible in turning your focus upon your mate? It is much greater, for you are closer. Perceiving the beautiful inner qualities of your beloved will have a tremendous effect. The results may not be immediate as with our stranger friend on the beach, but they

Beauty is everywhere —
only some can see it.

Confucius

will be long-lasting and deeply penetrating.

The opposite, of course, is also true. By focusing on your mate's negativity and weakness, you exert a powerful force that prevents both you and your partner from truly growing. A good rule for all committed couples is to avoid *idly* telling someone else the weaknesses of their mate. To reveal oneself to another is very special and should always be held in that light. To complain or grumble about your mate's weakness to another, without a constructive purpose, is to break that sacred trust. This not only has a negative effect upon your mate, but more so upon yourself. Criticism and judgment always backfire, and fill your own world with negativity.

Since 1979 I have held a women's meditation group in our home. We concentrate on different spiritual themes and work toward integrating that theme into our daily lives. One stormy night four women attended. After our meditation together I announced we would be working on feeling devotion for the closest male in our lives. Since all of us were in a relationship, I asked them to concentrate on their mates. Two women slightly grumbled, the third showed obvious dislike of the topic, and the fourth lit up with eager anticipation. Despite the resistance from the three women, I pushed on. I asked them to close their eyes and feel the deepest beauty of their mate, the quality they most loved.

The first woman, after some hesitation, described her husband as very solid. She was silent for a moment, then said, "Even though he doesn't always show it, he really does care about me." As she focused on this quality in him, her face softened. A light came into her eyes as she announced, "He really does love me." With that statement, a warmth permeated the room as we all felt this man and his quiet, unassuming love for his wife. His beauty was not dramatic, but rather inward and peaceful. When we thought of him, we all felt more peaceful and quiet inside.

The second woman then began slowly and sadly, "How much I have wanted to change my husband, to make him more spiritual and to initiate more affection toward me! But he doesn't do these things." Her face was full of sadness and sorrow for the qualities her husband did not have. She was silent a moment, then lightened and said, "He does respond when I love him." A smile came upon her too as she added, "Really he's like a flower opening to the sun whenever I pour out love to him. He smiles and delights in my love for him." As she spoke about him in this way, her face became like the sun and all present could feel her nourishing love.

We all knew her husband, but when she spoke about the quality of receptiveness, we saw him in an even deeper way. Even more beautiful was seeing this woman glow with love and strength. She sat for a moment, tears welling up in her eyes, and said, "He is so receptive to me. Here I've been resenting his lack of initative in loving me, not even seeing the privilege that is mine to help make him shine, and thus make myself shine. To him I am a channel of God's nourishing love. He needs that from me as much as I need to give that to him."

The third woman was obviously having discomfort with the entire exercise, and I knew she felt like running from the room. There was a darkness over her face as we all turned our attention upon her. She was having difficulties with her partner, and often felt like leaving him. She often doubted she was with the right person. With much sadness she sighed, "I really don't have anything beautiful to say about him." As she said this, her face dropped down, and there was very little light about her.

An awkward silence fell upon us all, until I asked her to look at me and try a little harder. She hesitantly admitted, "Well, he knows how to tell the weather." I asked her to explain, so she described his special attunement with the weather. Her face brightened as she conveyed his deep love of the elements, and how through this love he could feel his friend the rain coming days ahead of time. He tried to live a life inspired by the American Indians. We all became very enthusiastic and asked her to continue. She smiled broadly and said she had forgotten the beauty of that quality. She had been wanting him to fit her image of our husbands, and here he was, unique in his own beauty. As she talked more about this aspect of his being, she saw him in a fresh new way. Part of his way of loving and caring for her was to use his attunement to nature to bring forth exquisite beauty into their surroundings. His nurturing of their vegetable garden was a way of showing her how much he cared for her.

The woman then realized that this quality had attracted her in the first place. In time, her steadily increasing desires for him to be different were blocking her from seeing his unique beauty and contribution to the world. Then breathing freely she said, "My father has always told me I can see a glass as half empty or half full. I have been only seeing what my partner wasn't, rather than what he was." Her face, like the others before her, shone with inner peace.

With great joy the fourth woman told us how deeply she loved her husband. To her, his most beautiful quality was his willingness to serve others. She said he was always ready to give help to whoever needed it. Then she paused a moment and burst into tears saying, "Sometimes I think it's almost silly how much I love him. I'm almost thirty and we've been together for six years, yet I feel an overwhelming adoration for him. I feel like a child sometimes." She felt a little embarrassed by her tears and devotion. As she spoke a picture flashed before my mind, a memory of myself I had long since forgotten. It was a scene shortly after we were married. I shared it with the women:

Barry had a difficult time getting into medical school, so when a black school in the south accepted him, he readily went. In 1968 it was not easy to be a white minority in a black school in the south. There was much racial prejudice and, though the blacks were friendly toward Barry, he was always an outsider. The white community also rejected him for associating with the blacks.

We were married during Barry's Christmas break. The wedding had been so beautiful, as was our short honeymoon and trip down south. We found a cute little apartment, and with much joy fixed it up.

Soon it was the day to return to school. Barry didn't start until late morning, so we had a leisurely breakfast together. He then dressed in his school clothes and brought out his pile of books. His desire to be a doctor was very strong, yet medical school was one of the greatest challenges of his life thus far. I could tell that it was hard for him to return to a difficult school situation. He did not complain, yet sadness was written across his face. As I looked at him, something happened within me. It was as if my inner eyes were opened. I beheld Barry's greatness and saw how the difficulty of this situation was bringing out his deep inner beauty more and more. I had never felt more love for him than I did in that moment. I fumbled for words, not knowing how to express myself. Finally I simply said, "Barry, I feel in such awe of your beauty."

No one had ever said that to him before. He told me many years later, he didn't know at the time how to handle such love and adoration coming toward him. He just awkwardly said, "Oh gee, maybe you shouldn't feel that way." Five years later we had a spiritual counseling session with a gifted psychic friend and teacher. In the session, he said Barry had a profound experience in January of 1969. This experience had altered the course of his life and was his spiritual rebirth. Besides our wedding in late December, 1968, we could not remember anything unusual happening in the following month. He urged us to try to remember,

and several years later we did. It was that moment of my feeling awe and wonder for his beauty that had so changed Barry. It seemed so insignificant at the time, that both of us had forgotten. In one fleeting moment, God had used my eyes to show Barry who he really was, and he could never completely go back again to the old model.

This is what a master does for a disciple, constantly reflecting his or her real self. I was certainly no master, and at age 22 was rather immature in my spiritual outlook. But I innocently and completely loved Barry so much that God's creative power of love could come through and mirror to Barry his inner being and beauty.

Our little group sat silently for awhile. I had known these women for over five years, but had never felt closer to them than I did at that moment. There was a magical feeling in the air and we all felt it. By concentrating on the beauty of our companions, we had also awakened the beauty of the male part of ourselves. Each of us was shining a little more brightly because of it.

Can you see what a responsibility and joyful duty is ours to help each other grow, to mold each other's lives, and our own...like potter's clay!

There is always something beautiful to be found if you will look for it. Concentrate on beauty rather than on the reverse. This positive, loving attitude towards life and people is all part of the divine magic which we are endeavoring to reveal to you. It is helping you to perceive the divine Presence, helping you to put into operation the divine magic which heals.

WHITE EAGLE

eight

Making Love to God

It is God who is the One Loved in every loved one and it is He who loves through each lover the infinite reflections of the attributes of His perfection.

IBN L'ARABI

A book on love relationships would be incomplete without a section on sexuality. In truth, this whole book is about the sexual relationship, for in a conscious relationship it is artificial to separate the sexual from the total relationship. However, much can and needs to be said about sex. Most people have a difficult time with this aspect of their lives, but those traveling the spiritual path can develop unique problems in handling sexual energy.

Some of us assume we no longer have sexual desire, that we've outgrown it. Some of us feel hopelessly trapped on the other side: that sexual drives dominate our thinking and life. But most of us are somewhere in-between, alternating between one or the other polarity — either toward repression or toward over-indulgence.

The answer is not to be found in either extreme, but has to do with transformation. Sexual energy must eventually be transformed. Our concepts of good and evil, and the judgments we make, form the barrier. Sex is neither good nor bad. It is our limited way of thinking that makes it so. Simply stated, sexual energy *is*. Self-acceptance, which means honesty with ourselves about our experience, combined with open-mindedness, is one requirement for this transformation. Most of us know very well the all-consuming intensity of physical passion and deadness of sexual repression. In time, all of us can know the ecstatic merging experience where the sexual act is no less than a prayer of praise and thanksgiving.

Not long ago Joyce and I met a man who had obviously done much work on himself through traveling, studying, and practicing a number of spiritual disciplines. At one point, we were talking about sex, and how hard it is to make it conscious. Our friend was giving a lengthy discourse on "cosmic sex," the evolution of sexuality and his understanding of the topic, when I was suddenly struck by the realization that we can't have conscious physical sex unless we're open to the natural purpose of sex — the creation of a new body for a soul wanting to incarnate. This is not just intellectual agreement, but it means being completely awake to this truth during the sexual act. In this way sex becomes a more inclusive act. This doesn't mean everyone should try to conceive with every sexual act. But we can work to keep our hearts open to as many levels of sexuality as we can.

Sex can be a creative act — an act of creation. It can be the co-participation of a man and woman in bringing about the vehicle for a soul to join the human family, to learn mastery, and to help the planet. It can be an act of love, joining two beings, and *actually opening up a pathway to the heavens.*

There are women and a few couples who report similar experiences during that act of love-making which turns out later to conceive their child. They all describe a three-way link-up of energy — some see this visually while others feel or sense this connection. The bond or union between the couple would feel deeper than during previous sexual experiences, but in addition there would be a definite link established with a third being, often felt as overshadowing the couple. Some have described a great and masterful presence, while others sense the presence of a little child. One couple saw a being of great light who defied any description.

Are these hallucinations? We prefer to think not. We agree with those who speak about opening the door-way to heaven worlds, establishing a spiritual connection with the soul of the child. We feel there is a spiritual counterpart to physical conception — a loving contact with another being either consciously or unconsciously made by the couple in the process of uniting.

Besides the natural physical or reproductive level of sex, there is the level of communication — common union or sharing the spirit of love. One way our love-making can become a method for our awakening is by learning the secret of giving. The communion that we long for can only enter the sexual experience through the act of giving. This means thinking of our partner's happiness, even creating ways of giving pleasure to our partner. In fact, we can give the whole sexual experience as a gift to our partner and to God. Our joy will then be very great. But this can be tricky, for we have to sincerely desire to give. If we give expecting to later receive, we will fail.

In addition, many times we forget that one of the highest ways to give is to receive — to be receptive. Sometimes during the dance of love the greatest way to give joy is to allow our lover to give to us, and then to be open and sensitive to their gifts. It is easy to miss this if we lock ourselves into the notion that giving must mean doing or performing. Whether man or woman, real giving requires complete receptivity, like an open vessel deeply appreciating what is being poured into it, with a gentle acceptance that allows everything to be just as it is.

A couple once came for counseling to work on their "sexual" problem. In the session, it was soon apparent they had reached a level of loving commitment, but their sexual relationship seemed an insurmountable obstacle to them. They had been to a marriage counselor, and even a sex counselor. No matter how fair everyone tried to be, however, it always came out looking more like *her* problem: some deep emotional block causing frigidity. This only reinforced how they felt anyway.

After hearing their story we felt prompted to focus only on the man — to expose his half of the problem. One trick we've learned over the years counseling couples who present a mutually agreed upon one-sided problem: Somebody's gullible and somebody else is hiding. There's no such thing as an individual problem in committed lovers, two persons who have accepted the monogamous relationship as part of their path to God. However subtle this may be, an outwardly-appearing individual problem is a symptom of some deeper pathological dynamic in the couple. One partner's neurosis feeds the other's, but often the symptoms become more obvious in one person, as in the case of this couple.

Our focused attention upon this man was very hard for him, for he was accepted by both of them as the teacher and helper. He would have much preferred the three of us to try to help his wife with *her* problem. It took fancy pushing and some heavy moments, intermingled with just the right amount of cajoling and humor, before his heart could open to his equally-shared responsibility in *their* problem. What finally emerged was a subtle selfishness on his part. He was demanding sex on his own terms and for his own gratification, even though in a somewhat sensitive and gentle way.

According to many therapists this attitude might have been seen as normal and healthy. However, for a couple working to spiritualize their marriage as this couple was, it just does not work. Affirmation that we were on the right track was given by the woman. For as soon as her husband opened to his own feelings of inadequacy — his sexual greed — she became very attracted to him. As long as he was the sexual superman — having it all together — he was not attractive to her in a sensual way.

The question ultimately became clear: Did they want a shared orgasm, or did they want a feeling of love and openness to one another? As long as their attention was on the former they would miss the latter and she would be frigid anyway; which only means that she, like many women (as well as men), was failing at ''performing'' the sexual act devoid of love.

At these moments, both were losing the higher perspective. On an ego level this woman wanted desperately to perform — not only to feel sexually satisfied, but to satisfy her husband as well. Likewise, her husband longed for that pure embrace of lovers, longing to give himself completely to his wife.

It often happened that this couple would be sharing a loving moment together, perhaps sharing an inspiration after meditating together. Out of this spiritual togetherness in mind and feeling would come the natural desire for togetherness in body as well. Giving in to this desire they would hold each other and kiss, but at some point the energy would subtly shift. The desire for pleasure would pre-empt the desire for love and the peace of the moment would be lost. For him, giving would insidiously be replaced by taking. For her, the communion of giving and receiving would be replaced by performing. The one would now become two. Their unity would be lost, and their relationship would now become: "give me/do well (dual)."

Perhaps the most helpful thing of all for this couple was our honest sharing of our own continuing work on our sexual relationship. Every couple tends to feel that their problems are entirely unique, that they are the only ones in the world suffering in this way. Intellectually they may know this is not so, but a nagging doubt smolders in their feelings. What a relief to know other couples are sharing your most intimate problems!

We suggested to this couple a sexual moratorium, that together they make the decision not to have intercourse for a set period of time, within reason and agreeable to both. We also suggested they agree to not have orgasm by any method during this time period. We knew this couple's deeper intentions were good, but their achievement-oriented hang-up of attaining (and failing at) "that perfect orgasm together" was getting in the way.

A set period of abstinence, we have learned, can be a powerful tool in the work of transforming sexual energy — if each partner desires this transformation. If one partner grudgingly goes along with this decision, it cannot work for either. It can be likened to fasting. A well-planned fast can cleanse not only the body but the mind and feelings as well. Abstaining from food, or eating a mono-diet such as one kind of fruit, can also teach us much about our eating habits. Our awareness becomes sharpened so that after the fast we become more sensitive to *when* we need to eat and *what* our bodies need to eat. When a couple shares a fast together, their spiritual growth can be enhanced. Of course, it is possible for one spouse to fast alone, but this requires the utmost sensitivity toward the other spouse. We know a man who recently embarked upon an extended fast without consideration for his wife's feelings. He fasted. She ate. He became irritable and self-righteous. She withdrew, thinking not-too-wonderful things about her husband. The duration of the fast was a fiasco. They barely communicated. The whole purpose of the fast was sabotaged.

The same can apply to a sexual fast. Therefore, we encouraged our couple to allow themselves to feel attracted to one another without the pressure to engage in physical love-making. We encouraged them to explore the depths of their sexual feelings, to allow the flow of energy to course through their bodies rather than adopting an austere and self-righteous attitude and avoiding all sensuality.

With this couple willing to follow this simple advice the inevitable happened: in the days that followed they found themselves almost perpetually turned-on to each other. The man became much more considerate of his wife's feelings and needs. She discovered she was anything but frigid. She had never before in her life felt so much of a flow in her body — a real aliveness. The exercise taught them so much about the power of expectation, the way we subtly program our sexuality and our lives. It also taught them how much power and love is available by living in the present moment, rather than always being one step ahead of our actual experience.

Later we instructed them to resume their love-making, explaining that their recent experience had sensitized and sharpened their awareness. Their sexual moratorium had given them new tools to help show them when they moved into future programming — into orgasm consciousness. At times they found themselves slipping into their old habits: he gradually putting on the pressure and she gradually tightening up. Then one or both would wake up to what was happening and they could stop and relax into the present moment again, allowing the flow of love and openness to continue.

Open communication is essential for a conscious sexual relationship. This doesn't necessarily mean talking out every step of the way, although in some cases it may. It means an honest sharing of all of you — being vulnerable and visible. It may mean keeping your eyes open, sharing without any words. Open communication requires sensitivity to the feelings and experience of your mate. It's so easy to become preoccupied with your own experience, whether it is during sex or any other time. But it is very possible to rise above this selfishness. It is possible, as many of us have experienced, for the flow of love to become so strong even at the point of orgasm that we stop the whole physical process to just look into each other's eyes or express our love in words. The orgasm has become unimportant — even irrelevant. It is as if the sexual feelings transcend the genitals and encompass the whole body. From there, the experience can then move to higher and higher levels of consciousness, adding new dimensions of ecstatic joy and gratitude. Human sex can become a union of the highest order.

Some years ago, Joyce and I had to pass through a phase of over-zealousness in regards to spiritualizing our sexual relationship. We insisted that every episode of love-making be a perfect Divine Communion. Therefore we had to wait for just the right moment. We found that late at night, or when we were tired, we would lose consciousness too easily. Our physical, sensual passions would run rampant. So we forced ourselves to abstain at those times. When we woke up in the morning we would sometimes be really attracted to each other, but no, we wouldn't be "awake" enough. During the day we were often too busy. When we finally did have time alone, first we'd do our "spiritual" practices separately, then together and, when we started feeling close to how we thought we should, our time alone was used up!

We were afraid of failing at "spiritual sex." We almost stopped touching each other completely. Yet, the truth of the matter was we were suppressing our desire and attraction for one another. We were viewing sexual desire as "unholy" — a human weakness that had no relation to God.

In reality, there is nothing unholy about sexual energy, just like there is nothing unholy about any energy. All energy is of God, but as human beings we have free will to express this Divine Energy in any way we want, ways that will either help or hurt, not only us, but all life as well.

Joyce tells the story of how she and I came to this truth:

As I committed myself more deeply to the spiritual path I strongly desired to live a pure and holy life. I read and studied much about God and somehow conjured in my mind an image of the "holy woman" I wanted to become. This being was pure in every way and had nothing to do with sex. I began patterning my life after this image. I think most of us go through this stage at one time or another, trying very hard to act a part rather than simply accepting who we are.

I began throwing away all of my clothes that were at all revealing, replacing them with rather baggy "holy garb" that fit my new role. Barry also was trying out a similar new image, so together we agreed to control our sexual urges toward one another. We meditated more and began to clean up all areas of our life. It felt generally good. However, sometimes the desire for sexual union would overcome us and we'd feel much guilt after yielding to these feelings. I began to develop severe headaches which would be most acute whenever I would see a man in counseling. This became so unbearable that I stopped counseling men altogether. I also started getting sick much more than usual. Something just wasn't quite right and I didn't know what.

I decided to seek the advice of a beloved male teacher who was temporarily living several miles from us. I felt very nervous about going to see him and almost cancelled the appointment several times, but my inner feeling overwhelmingly urged me to go. I felt almost pushed out the door by an unseen hand. Arriving at his house early, I decided to sit in my car and pray for help to understand what I was doing wrong. After I said my prayer I felt fear surge through me. Something was rising within me. It was as if a volcano were about to erupt within me. I felt driven to the point of panic. I could hardly move. Somehow I made it from my car to his door, to a seat where our counseling session began.

He must have sensed my problem right away, for he began talking about sex and asked about my feelings. With some degree of pride I related how much work I had done on that one, and now felt almost done with those passions. (How grandly we judge our own progress sometimes!) He smiled a delightful smile and continued to question me. Then he looked at me a long time and asked how I was feeling. The panic once again rose within me. I felt as if something awful was about to burst forth. All attempts to hold this back were futile. As I sat there struggling with my body, I heard him speaking to me: "It's alright to feel attraction. When used properly sex is spiritual too."

A year's pent-up energy burst forth as I allowed myself to feel attracted to him, to feel a flow within my body. The energy was so strong I could have floated to the ceiling. What a beautiful feeling! I felt high in my body and at the same time felt God's Presence strongly. Sitting there I thought of Barry and felt so much love for him. The attractiveness, the sexual flow, was an integral part of our relationship and could serve to bring us into God's Presence as well as the other spiritual practices we were doing. To cut off our sexual energy prematurely is to cut off a vital force which can help bring spiritual union.

As I sat with this man who helped to awaken my heart to God many years ago, I felt so very grateful. It was alright to feel attracted to him or anyone, and let the energy flow through my body. The important thing is to recognize this magnetic pull as a part of loving another person. It is not at all necessary to act upon the feeling. It is enough to let it be.

The result of that experience was transforming. Barry felt the change in me instantly and this helped him to open also. My energy increased. I felt able to resume seeing men in counseling. The best part was that I felt an expanding love for Barry and a closer contact with God. The years of practiced control and at times celibacy were very necessary to help bring into balance the right use of sexual energy. It turned out to be a positive and valuable cycle in our relationship.

On the other hand, when sex is indulged in, or used outside of the relationship, it delays the couple's union in love. When used with a sense of reverence, it can help bring about a deeper spiritual merging. We can all feel the effects of this throughout our entire life. The energy of attractiveness can serve to open our hearts to all beings. This flow through the body can free us to receive more of God's love and light. We can allow the sexual energy to exist, yet we can also work to bring it more and more into the spirit of God's love, transforming it from the physical into the Divine.

PRACTICE

This practice is for committed couples. Sit in front of each other as closely as possible without touching. Close your eyes, tune into yourself, and relax each part of your body. Breathe slowly and deeply through each part of your body. Don't hurry this part. The rest of the exercise depends on adequate preparation. But also, don't get down on yourself for having a racing mind or tight body. Just do as much as you can, asking inside for peace and love.

Now open your eyes and take each other's hands. Look into your mate's eyes with gentleness and love, and breathe love back and forth with each breath. If you wish, visualize a ray of light connecting your hearts growing brighter with each conscious breath.

Next, remember a time when you felt the most deeply attracted to each other. Pick a specific time or event that stands out in your memory; a time you felt like a human magnet, so drawn were you to the beauty manifested in your mate.

Finally, and most important, feel how all this is still happening. It isn't just a memory. But perhaps this wonderful attraction has become somewhat covered up with day-to-day living. Perhaps you feel, as many of us tend to do on the spiritual path, that the physical attraction is less important than the other ways of connecting with each other. But can you begin to see how physical attraction is also part of the spark of love, and one part of the spark is no less important than any other. And if that special flow of love that passes as a current through your body is cut off, so also is the life in your body cut off to the same degree.

So go ahead, feel your attraction for this lovely being in front of you. Feel it in every cell of your body. Ground your love into the fullness of your being, even down to your toes. Keep opening to these feelings of pull, of yearning to merge, to join in love one with the other. Only by so doing will you learn what this attraction really is — not just with your mind.

Feel your physical attraction, for it is the earthly manifestation of your longing for the Heavenly Condition. It is the physical expression of Divine Love-making. Allowing sexual feelings to flow through your body, if they are unselfish, can open your heart to feelings of ecstatic joy, to sublime feelings of reverence. You find that these feelings cannot really be separated — that they all flow together.

Look deeply into the eyes of your beloved. Without moving a muscle, join every part of your being with him or her. Let your essence merge with that of your beloved. Make love to God!

As the love relationship deepens, and especially after having children, many women experience a decreasing desire for the purely physical aspect of sex. I have counseled many women who were afraid they had lost their desire altogether. One woman, an extreme case, shared how she was in the habit of going to sleep hours before her husband to avoid all possibility of sexual contact. This was causing great turmoil in a marriage that was otherwise very stable and strong. Some women have come to me feeling they have a very grave problem: they no longer feel strong sexual urges. Other women blame their mate, feeling a loss of tenderness and caring from him.

The truth is that neither one has a problem, has lost something, or is at fault. Sexual feelings change for both women and men and move to a different level. This may be simply the result of maturing, of giving birth and nursing, or of moving consciousness to a deeper spiritual level. What used to turn you on no longer does. Sex can transform a physical, passionate act into a profound spiritual experience with your partner. When approached in this way, the sexual act is more meaningful and fulfilling than ever before. Before, it was what your mate did to you that turned you on. Now it's what your mate is that turns you on! You need to flow with the spiritual aspect of your mate as well as the physical.

In the early years of a relationship sex is often approached in a purely sensual way. In time, the experience needs to broaden into new dimensions. Attractiveness changes along with consciousness. The more radiant your hearts are, the more attractive you become to each other. As you mutually touch the golden thread which unites your souls, your bodies respond in beauty and rhythm. The peak of sexual union is not the orgasm as before, but the deepening of love and respect for each other as you are catapulted into a higher union with your Source.

As we grow together as couples in love, we realize there is a higher purpose to sex. Behind our body and personality each one of us is both male and female. Sexual desire arises from this divided consciousness of man and woman longing for union, a divine dance being played out by two bodies. Sex in its highest function is an instrument for waking us up to our real oneness of Spirit. It can be a vehicle for reminding us of our original condition: the essential oneness of male and female. Even for those having no interest in the spiritual dimensions of sexuality, the orgasm is a tangible spiritual force that temporarily suspends ego functioning and gives an ecstatic taste of union with all existence.

Unfortunately, this taste and the resulting hunger are too often associated with the physical act of sex. We all tend to confuse the method with the goal, forgetting that the goal has to be brought into the method for it to work. In other words, we all long for this feeling of union, of oneness, which is a spiritual condition. The physical, sensual act of sex will never bring us this unless we imbue it with what we really desire. To go a step further, if our personal desire is not in tune with God's desire in us, we will again fall short. If our desire is selfish, if we desire union or bliss or a "high" only *for ourselves*, we might gain a pleasurable momentary experience, but ultimately we will be disappointed because our spiritual appetite has not been filled.

To allow sex its highest expression, we have to remember the true nature of desire. Moment to moment we have to choose. Are we desiring a release of tension? An intensity of physical pleasure? Or are we desiring to live out on the physical level a union between two beings that is really between soul and Spirit within each? Our deepest desire is for that Oneness, our original divine condition.

We also need to remember who it really is that we're making love with. Sex can be as expansive as we allow it to be. We can make love to someone's body. We can make love to their mind and personality. *Or we can make love to God, the essence of beauty and wisdom manifesting as two persons.* In this sense we are also making love to ourselves.

Since we're human, we must allow room for our human sexual desires. We need to be very honest with ourselves. At the same time we need to remember the spiritual reality. If we can hold to our desire for love, for Oneness, for God, then our human sexual relationship will become a profound spiritual experience.

A PRACTICE FOR LOVE-MAKING

Help us, Oh God, to merge our hearts and souls
as we now merge our bodies together.

Love-making can be a vehicle for experiencing the merging of two beings — when treated with reverence and respect. Over-indulgence will not bring about peak experiences in sex. If your favorite food is chocolate ice cream and you eat it every day, it loses some of its specialness and soon becomes routine. If you then decided to have it only once a week, however, or maybe once a month, how much more of a treat it would become. To some degree love-making is the same.

The first step in this practice, therefore, is for both of you to think of the sexual act with reverence — to bring it into your spiritual life — and not to abuse it, or each other. Both partners must agree to wait for the energy to be right. This takes patience, love and respect for the other's feeling and space. Pushing the other into having sex may bring about physical gratification or a release of tension, but can never bring about the peak experience: the merging of two consciousnesses into one.

Allowing for the right energy to exist between you for love-making is as much a spontaneous act as it is a planned event. One can plan just so much, and then there must be an openness for what is happening in the moment. Overly-rigid planning can result in disharmony and disappointment — or a forced physical act. I remember when we felt an inner prompting to travel to Mt. Shasta to conceive our second child. I had felt so inspired. The vision and essence of Mira had filled me with wonder and beauty. Then, however, my mind began planning the "event." I decided it would be just perfect to conceive her on New Year's Eve following the traditional group meditation. What I did not anticipate was how much the trip would tire us, that Barry would develop a headache, and that the energy for love-making just wasn't there between us on that night. I was disappointed and disharmony resulted. Several days later, however, Mira was conceived in spontaneous love and joy.

After waiting patiently and respectfully for a mutual agreement on love-making and a flow of loving energy has developed between you, the second step is to sit together and allow your minds to expand to a higher consciousness. It is usually hard to go from business phone calls or dirty diapers right into a high sexual experience. Your bodies may be ready, but your minds also have to be prepared together. You might sit in meditation together and allow your minds to go from their small worlds into the higher mind or expanded consciousness. Other suggestions are singing together, reading a special book out loud to each other, or your own unique way of feeling the higher purpose for your being here on earth. Afterwards, take the time to see and appreciate each other's beauty. By seeing more deeply into your partner's beauty, you are experiencing your own beauty.

As the last part of your preparation, offer a prayer together. Pray that your hearts and souls may be merged as your bodies become merged. Pray for help to surrender the experience to God. This is perhaps the most important part of love-making — and the most neglected. The deepest desire behind wanting to have sex is to become one with another totally — body, mind and spirit. This cannot fully happen without Divine Love and Help, for it is to the plane of God consciousness that you are wanting to rise.

Now feel your trust for each other. To have a best friend who you can totally trust and can share yourself completely is one of the greatest blessings of our human existence. Through deep trust and love you can rise together into higher and higher planes of consciousness not only in the sexual act but in all of life as well. This is the true beauty of the monogamous relationship. The sexual act in a deeply committed couple can be so sacred that it carries them into an ecstatic union.

Finally, let your bodies begin to flow together. Try not to get caught only in the physical passion, but concentrate instead on giving, expanding and merging. At some point towards the peak of your experience, before orgasm, be very still in mind and body. Stop all physical movement and use the energy to transcend your bodies, to expand your awareness. Allow yourselves to fly together into the light and to experience your Oneness. Feel with every ounce of your being how much you love each other, how much you love yourself, how much you love God, how united you are! Invite God into this experience and feel how very, very loved you are. Such moments can greatly enrich your relationship. Now, as you complete the sexual act, whether it goes on to orgasm or not, feel thankful for each other and for the privilege of so much love in your life.

The glory of friendship is not the outstretched hand, nor the kindly smile, nor the joy of companionship; it is the spiritual inspiration that comes to one when he discovers that someone else believes in him and is willing to trust him.

RALPH WALDO EMERSON

nine

The Higher/Lower Game

If I speak in the tongues of men and of angels, but have not love, I am a noisy gong or a clanging cymbal. And if I have prophetic powers, and understand all mysteries and all knowledge...but have not love, I am nothing.

I CORINTHIANS 13

There is a peculiar syndrome in couples where one person, more or less unconsciously, assumes the role of guru or teacher. I remember first encountering this in couples we knew in our psychological and psychiatric training: one person was the self-chosen therapist for the other, always of course unsatisfactorily. Our non-professional friends, as well, seemed to be playing this same game which transactional analysis calls the "parent-child" relationship. This is tricky, however, because underneath the obvious parent-child relationship, the "parent" is often more of a "child" than the "child." Moreover, by looking deeper into the "teacher-student" couple, the "student" quite often has more to teach than the "teacher."

The higher/lower game is illustrated perfectly by a couple we knew some years back. The man was middle-aged, with extensive academic credentials, and spoke beautifully on the nature of love and relationships. One of his students was a young woman in her early twenties. Eventually they entered a romantic relationship with each other, but she was always in the background — in his shadow. He was very charismatic and outgoing. She could hardly say a word. There were very few, indeed, who saw the loving smile playing around her lips, and even fewer who noticed the brightness of the light in her eyes. She was the example! She was living what he was talking about. We learned more about love looking into this young woman's eyes, with maybe a word here and a nod there, than we did from the elaborate discourses given by the man. She had so much to teach him, but he could not at the time open to her silent wisdom.

Joyce and I have always had our higher/lower game, too. We met at the age of eighteen, freshmen in college, with little real awareness of the deeper laws of life. I was hardly her guru at the time. Later, however, with my training in psychotherapy in medical school and then psychiatry, my seeds of inferiority sprouted their leaves of superiority! Thank God I was married to a strong woman who has loved me enough through the years to not let me get away with these distancing games.

Currently we each take turns feeling superior in very subtle ways. When it comes to emotions, sometimes I look like an idiot who doesn't feel anything. At those times it is hard for Joyce to catch in herself that subtle feeling of superiority. In intellectual areas, Joyce sometimes appears lacking, and I find myself judging her. Outwardly, there are these seeming strengths and weaknesses, but in reality this is not so. We are discovering that we each have just as little (or much) mastery in each of these areas of our life, but with different styles.

For example, in an argument where our emotions are disturbed, I (and many men) often lose control on the one pole of repression: "Who, me angry?" My emotions are upset and visible to anyone and everyone — except me. On the other pole, Joyce, and many women, often lose control in overexpression, or over-identification, sometimes feeling overwhelmed by turbulent emotions. In some couples this polarity is reversed: the woman represses while the man overexpresses emotion. It is interesting to see how one side creates the opposite side.

The same holds true for intellectual functioning. In areas of rational thinking or knowledgeability I may subtly judge myself superior. However, in areas of interest to Joyce, her thought has far greater depth and clarity than mine.

Gradually, we are learning a very important lesson; the letting go of competition, one of the greatest stumbling blocks in the love relationship. We all suffer from this condition in varying degrees. We learn to compete with each other very early in life — to win love and recognition by coming out better. Then we find that by winning in our relationships we are really losing. In order to feel "better" than our friend, we have to make him or her an object, and this pulls us out of love. Love is only possible with unification, with expanding the horizon of our being to include another being or beings. Love transforms competition. The relationship journey eventually teaches us that *OUR* emotions become disturbed, rather than yours or mine. The individual manifestations of the disturbance become less important than the overall disturbance to a couple united in love. Blame and judgment have no power in this higher perspective. It becomes much easier to solve problems, because two minds and two hearts are working together rather than against each other.

The Boyfriend in "Samadhi"*

The "Higher/Lower Game" is also illustrated by two other couples who came to us for counseling. The first couple also demonstrates how wonderfully true lovers are sometimes brought together. The man was older, which in itself often encourages a superior attitude. In his meditations and visualizations at times the face of a young woman would flash before his inner vision. It was always the same face, someone he had no memory of meeting. One night he was attending a lecture at a university, and found two vacant chairs right up front. He took one of them, and having arrived early, closed his eyes for a brief meditation.

Meanwhile, a young woman arrived at the same lecture. All day she had been experiencing an unusual premonition that something wonderful was soon to take place, but what it was she did not know. As she entered the auditorium, a very strange thing

*A Sanscrit term denoting certain high states of consciousness

happened. She felt herself pulled toward the front row by some force that she could barely control. This would have all seemed very normal, except that her route to the front, hardly by her choice, was directly over and through the set up chairs, creating havoc, with chairs crashing to the floor! Finally, with a resounding thump, she landed on the vacant seat in the front, next to this man, who was almost too embarrassed to open his eyes. But when he did, there beside him was the woman of his vision! They spent the whole lecture gazing into each others' eyes, and that was that.

Well, not quite. They still had a bit of a problem, which several months later caused the woman to set up an appointment with Joyce and me. In the session she explained how much of a drag she was on their relationship. When we asked her to describe her boyfriend, she stated matter-of-factly, "He's in Samadhi all the time." While she was talking, we happened to look out the window and saw him sitting in his car, appearing slightly bored.

We said, "No!"

She said, "Yes...at least that's what he says."

"What do you feel?" we asked.

"Well," she replied, "I'm not sure. But he seems to be so much more together than me in every way."

Viewing the relationship from a superficial level, he did seem to have it very together. But we knew this wasn't so. Something smelled a little bit fishy to us. Knowing the story of their meeting, we knew without a doubt that these two souls shared the same level of inner growth, but with differing outward lessons to learn. When we shared our feeling with her, she became very happy, for it resonated with that deep place in her that knew this to be true.

Since she didn't drive, her boyfriend would bring her each time for her appointment. At first we noticed he sat in his car, reading, meditating...or being bored. Later, he seemed to be sitting closer and closer to the house each time. Finally, he asked if he could be a part of what was happening with the three of us. So the next visit he was included. It wasn't an easy session. It's never easy when a person thinks they're more advanced on the spiritual path than they really are. However, after receiving help inwardly, Joyce and I ended up laughing at him so hard, and his heart was opened just enough, that he too saw the humor of the situation.

From then on, the four of us could work together with real openness and clarity. Time after time, however, we had to catch him in his teacher role, and her in her disciple role. Nevertheless, it was a privilege for Joyce and me to work with such a close couple, helping them through their ups and downs together.

From Pedestal to Pit

The second couple was tougher. The man had become quite well known in spiritual circles. He possessed the gift of attuning to a higher level of consciousness in front of audiences, transcending his personality level, and inspiring many persons. His wife was one of his students, who from the beginning placed him on such a high pedestal that she was blind to his human nature for a long time. He would do his thing and she would swoon!

However, the Divine Power that draws two people together is not fooled by apparent differences in spiritual advancement. The chemistry of love knows only equality — equal giving and receiving — each soul having just as much to learn as the other has to teach. Hence this woman, after marriage, experienced a tremendous let down. "Prince Charming" many times appeared to be more of a frog than a prince. One by one, different obnoxious personality traits popped out, each one seeming harder to bear than the previous one. Finally, even when he was doing his "spiritual thing," she couldn't see past the personal interaction they were developing. In her eyes he had gone from pedestal to pit.

In our first meeting together, she complained to Joyce and me that she didn't know such a great spiritual leader would turn out to be so "spaced out," unfeeling, and inconsiderate. Our guru-friend, in turn, admitted his surprise that this woman whose devotion and love seemed to flow out in unending torrents, had turned out to be a complaining nag. Sparks started to fly! Eventually, we needed to separate them: Joyce taking the woman to another room, while I remained with the man.

In this case the couple had reached a point where they just could not be themselves in each other's presence. This happens at times with every couple, until a deep enough level of commitment and trust is developed. To have kept them together trying to work through the hostility might have been slow and laborious, or might have even further closed their hearts to each other. We have found that temporary one-on-one relating at this point can often more quickly bring each partner to a deeper level of seeing and feeling. The personality interference that occurs while together can be like loud static on a radio preventing each from hearing/feeling perceptions and deeper feelings. Feelings of sadness, fear, or inadequacy remain covered up by the "static" of anger, pride, and judgment.

Our first task with each person was to simply quiet the unproductive babble of negativity. This was fairly easy now that they were separated from one another. If we were to allow these two to verbalize their negative feelings and thoughts toward each other, it would have been an unending stream of projection or blame.

In other couples, one or both persons may be unaware of their negativity toward the other. This hidden negativity can cause even greater tension between the two. Individual therapy with each partner in this case would consist of first drawing out this hidden tension — possibly in the form of anger or resentment. By carefully listening and feeling, a therapist can determine the direction the person is most resisting, and therefore most needing to confront. If you as a therapist listen only to the words, the content, you get lost in your client's drama. If you don't listen enough to the words as a human being, he or she will be alienated and may react to you as not being with them. You learn to be there with all of you, hearing deeply everything they say, but hearing most of all what they are needing to say. This can be done only with enough love which, when present, allows the person a real opportunity for transformation.

While I was alone with this man, his work became clear. His heart was closed to his wife's beauty, which is to say, he had closed to his inner female nature. Consequently, he was too much in his head (his intellect), resulting in a hardness, coldness, sharpness, but also an arrogance and unawareness of his sadness that caused him to feel superior. He was conscious, however, of a yearning for the mother aspect of God, the Divine Mother, but he hadn't yet put that together with his wife and inner woman. It's all one yearning! As soon as a man accepts and acknowledges the woman within himself — that he is also a she — he is becoming one with his wife and the Mother God, and he softens, warms, and becomes aware of his feelings.

My work with this man was to zero in on his female side. He was stuck in his masculinity, which I proceeded to ignore. I encouraged him to share with me the most beautiful qualities of his wife, those qualities that had attracted him to her in the first place. I had to push him very hard. The ego rebels strongly against this opening of the heart, for it spells death. Yet the ego must go through this death experience, often accompanied by pain, prior to the opening of the heart. Often, this must happen to us a number of times in different ways, to impress us deeply of our folly, and the real process of life. But oh what a reward!

Finally, this man welled up with tears. His heart was open. He saw the connection. He just never realized that what he was fighting against the hardest, what he was pushing away the most, was the very thing he was most wanting.

Meanwhile, in the other room, a similar process was needing to happen with the woman. Her heart was needing to open to the beauty and goodness of her husband, representative of the male aspect of God, the father principle...the perfection of her own innate maleness. Through her relationship with this man, her naive illusions were shattered. Painful, yes, but now an integration could take place, a true meeting and merging of male and female.

I don't know what has become of this couple, but I do know that if ever they get lost into the same games of projection, their suffering will probably be deeper. For each time a person contacts the truth, each time one sees through the mist, he or she becomes more sensitive to the untruths of their lives. Although their suffering may deepen, so will *they* deepen, and their joy and vision will rise to greater heights.

A woman once wrote Joyce a letter as a result of reading our column on relationships in a local paper. It illustrates, together with Joyce's answer, the "other side of the coin":

"Dear Joyce,
I have been with my husband now for six years. I'm thinking seriously of leaving him. Deep down I think I really love him, but am heartsick over the hopelessness of the situation. I started meditating a little over three years ago and have filled my life more and more with spiritual pursuits. It seems that as I've done this, my husband has gone in the opposite direction, living more and more of a materialistic life. I know he resents all that I am doing, and seems to do everything he can to stop me. I am afraid that my growth is blocked by my staying with him, but if I leave him, am I running away from my karma? Please, what do you feel about all this?"

Joyce answers:

How often in our counseling experiences do we see a problem just like yours. It seems to be one of many tests that people face as they journey on the spiritual path. Sometimes the awakening process will quicken the heart of one partner first, at least for a time. Let's look at the woman for example, as in your case.

In her yearning for God, she may plunge herself into spiritual practices. After a time she will look over at her husband, who is perhaps growing just as fast but in other ways. However, since he isn't meditating or working with the outward spiritual forms, it seems to the woman that she is leaving him behind. If she starts to feel superior to the man, he will react and may go in the opposite direction, rejecting anything spiritual. If the woman tried to push her practices on him, likewise will he react. I have seen all too many potentially beautiful relationships break up at this point.

Then what are you to do? I know it can be a very painful situation for you. First, it is important to know that we are drawn to a partner because of spiritual balance. It is the need of our soul to be

drawn to one who will help us grow in every way. Unless you are a very, very advanced soul, like perhaps Ramakrishna and his disciple-wife Sarada Devi, you will be drawn to one who is at the same level of advancement as you. Try to remember what attracted you in the first place to this being...remember those early feelings. If you can be really honest with yourself, you will remember that he stirred your soul to inspiration by the love that you both felt. Can you remember how he seemed so ideal, and his beautiful qualities seemed to jump out at you? Well, they are still there. They haven't gone anyplace. We get into ruts about how we see people, especially our mates. The spiritual beauty is still there. It is our job to focus upon that, and by our attention and love to draw that out. That is perhaps one of the most important spiritual practices you could do right now. As you feel his real inner nature, you will make him want to become all that you feel and see. As you love and see his spiritual side, you bring it out more and more. And as this process evolves, you will notice a change in yourself.

Your husband is a reflection of your own maleness. If you think negatively about him, so in turn are you thinking negatively about yourself. Those who can see clearly tell us that two-thirds of a thought toward another stays to act in our own world. So if you can think positively about him and see who he really is, you will be drawing out your own spiritual beauty. Then you will be following one of the greatest of all commandments...to love one another.

When we start out on our journey of awakening, we think in terms of this practice and that practice — and we judge our progress (and others' progress) by how well we or they are doing the practices. Perhaps your husband is right now serving as your greatest spiritual teacher, and your loving him unconditionally will take you over a step you might not be able to go alone.

In your times alone, pray to feel his real inner self, his beauty. Visualize his beauty. Only then will you be shown whether you are to stay together or not. But regardless, you will be helping both of you to progress on the path.

The following story illustrates the "higher/lower game" in our own relationship, as well as showing how this kind of destructive energy can be healed:

One spring I elected to take a weekend course on healing to comply with the continuing education requirements for renewal of my nursing license. I wasn't particularly looking forward to this course, but I was looking forward to a weekend away from Barry. Barry and I were in a rather low phase of relating. He was gone alot from home either working at the hospital or counseling. I had been home writing and meditating. It seemed to me that he was losing a certain spiritual sensitivity. As my sensitivity grew from being alone, his seemed to lesson with each day. I began to see Barry as spacy, materialistic, and worst of all, I began to feel spiritually superior.

The course was to be held at a beautiful conference spot on the ocean near Monterey. As I was packing up I had the strangest feeling I would meet and fall in love with a new man during the course of the weekend. This feeling disturbed me as I hadn't had the slightest interest in any other man in over ten years. I tried to push away the feeling of excitement and anticipation over meeting this new man, but it would come back all the stronger, and so I just let it be.

The Friday afternoon of my departure came and Barry and I spent a warm and loving time together before I left. I felt close to him — but it just wasn't the closeness that we can feel. He still seemed slightly spacy to me and I still felt slightly superior in my meditative stillness of mind. Barry and Rami had great plans for the weekend and there were many hugs and kisses as I drove off. As I caught one last look at my two beloveds, the thought of meeting this new man pierced me like an arrow.

The course discussed healing through our minds and how the body is giving us signals on how we should change our lives. As I walked into the conference room, I quickly looked through the room at the participants. Of the forty people present, only seven were men and most were over fifty years old. None seemed very appealing to me from a romantic viewpoint. I sat down with relief and felt that my intuitive sense about meeting this new person had been wrong.

During the next three days the leader of the course took us through a series of meditative exercises which were all designed for healing. He had asked us to pick out one area of our life that needed healing. Most participants needed healing of the body. I felt my main area of healing needed to be my relationship with Barry. Though ours was already a beautiful relationship, I was ever aware of the weaker areas between us. I wanted to stop seeing Barry as spacy. Most of all, I wanted to stop feeling superior.

As we were instructed during the exercises, I placed before my inner guide and healer my problem and asked for guidance. The answer repeatedly came to concentrate on Barry's beauty, to let go of his weaker areas and see his goodness; to let go of the ways his being isn't so spiritual and to see the deep spiritual nature that is already there. We did this exercise five times as a group, each time going a little deeper. The first time I had to work on just letting go of seeing Barry as spacy. It took deep concentration to remember and feel his spiritual side. Then as we progressed in the course it became easy to let go of his weaker areas and his beauty began to emerge more and more. Through the meditative process I saw Barry in ways I had rarely seen. The rays of spiritual light were pouring forth from his heart, and I felt deep remorse at ever having felt superior to his being. I felt how equal we are and going beyond that, our oneness.

Barry once again became my beloved, my other half, my helper to greater light. I felt so much love and devotion for Barry I could hardly contain myself. The love I felt for him spilled out into every area of my life. I felt love for every one at the conference and my body felt alive and glowing. I just couldn't wait to see him, so I called and invited him down to join us for the last morning. He agreed!

Sunday morning came and I tingled with eagerness to be reunited with my beloved. It had been less than 48 hours since I had said good-bye and here I was eager to see him again. During the morning break I sat outside hoping Barry would come. Then there he was! His outer appearance hadn't changed one bit. Two days ago I would have probably still labeled him as spacy. But now he was the most beautiful sight in the world to me because my perception of him had changed on the inside. I ran into his arms and we hugged and kissed. I felt reunited with my beloved and it was just heavenly. The changes I saw and felt weren't in him — they had been in how I had chosen to see and experience him. I was so proud to introduce him to the new friends I had met. One sweet, older lady felt for certain we were on our honeymoon. I looked at Barry then and knew that he was the new man I was to meet — and once again fall in love with.

PRACTICE

---

*(also recommended for individual meditations,
visualizing your partner)*

Sit facing each other for this exercise. Start by closing your eyes to get more in tune with yourself. Calm your energies.

When ready, open your eyes and make contact with each other. Again, don't just sit and stare at each other; that accomplishes nothing. Look just as much at yourself as at the person in front of you. Relax...be natural.

Now for the man: feel within yourself all that is fatherlike, the strength that you may have only rarely experienced, the power of God that is at the same time gentle as it is strong. Feel that part of you that wants to protect this woman in front of you. All men have this quality, though it may be more submerged in some. Go ahead. Feel this. Your acknowledgement will help in the manifestation of this aspect of your relationship.

For the woman at the same time: accept and feel the little girl, the child within you that wants, and needs, the love of the Father. Go a bit further; open yourself and receive (with joy and gratitude) this strength, this protection, and love. For just as he attunes to the father aspect of God within him, so also will you. For by loving and receiving the highest aspect of maleness that comes through your lover, you will learn to know this same power of the Father within yourself.

This is one of the exquisitely beautiful lessons a man and woman can learn through their relationship.

Now for the reverse. We'll start with the woman: feel and accept all that is motherliness within you, a great love and tenderness that wants to reach out and enfold the little boy in front of you. Yes, this also is happening in every woman.

And for the man: feel that little boy part of you that longs to be held and loved and nourished by your Mother, manifesting as this woman in front of you. Open yourself now and receive all this from her, and Her. For the Mother-God within you can be made visible in the one sitting in front of you. You may want to rebel, to run away and hide, but ultimately you must accept your need for your Mother-God.

When this child within you both coexists in peace with the Mother-Father within you, when you are open to the power, wisdom, and love within you and at the same time open to the yearning and need for these qualities, then you will be humble. And in your humbleness, you will know infinite gratefulness for each other and for all the blessings of life.

ten

The Care and Feeding of Couples

Behind every 'O Lord' of thine, are a thousand ''Here am I's''

MEVLANA JELALU'DDIN RUMI

A growing, enduring relationship must be continually replenished. Like any living thing that needs water and food, the bond of friendship between two persons is really very delicate. It can easily wither and die without proper nourishment, which comes in the form of renewed inspiration and support.

I remember a couple who came to us some time ago for counseling. They were both very sincere seekers of truth who came together powerfully into a relationship. However, their living situation was far from ideal: a house full of single people. Not only did they lack support for being a couple, but they were even the target of subtly-negative comments and even outright resentment. They were aware enough to see the jealousy and desire in their housemates, but they were not strong enough to withstand the force of negativity directed at them. By the time they came to see us they were feeling many doubts about the validity of being in a relationship. None of their friends had anything good to say about it. It turned out, in their case, that they benefited from just being with another couple who believed in the beauty of shared love. As soon as they moved into a house of their own, things improved.

In the world today, there seems to be a wide-spread pessimism about the committed love relationship. There seems to be an accumulated force of doubt and fear coming out of misunderstood hurts and painful failures. Those of us who are in many ways naive and simple, and hold a vision of walking all life's paths hand-in-hand with our beloved, of merging two hearts into the one heart of God, are under constant attack from these forces within and without. Our vision is so easily buried by doubts and fears.

We cannot do it alone! No matter how strong our bond of love, it will either calcify into routines and expectations, or be severed by the axe of fear when the fire gets too intense. Couples who want a living spiritual relationship must learn to recognize the need for help. The two of us have needed *so much* help since we met in 1964. I think we are even more aware of our need now.

Couples on the spiritual path very deeply need to be with couples pursuing the same goals. In a conscious relationship we're not just wanting to coexist, we're wanting to merge into one being, to learn perfect unconditional love, to become the gentle balance of male and female. Like the biblical statement, "When two or more are gathered in my name (God), there I am," the same goes for couples. When two or more couples meet in the spirit of love — praying, singing, meditating, sharing the journey together — in their midst will reside the Divine Couple: the prototype of the relationship, blessing and strengthening all present.

There is a group of committed couples which meets periodically at our house in the evening. We all recognize our need for inspiration and the rededication of our relationships. Our whole purpose for meeting is to illumine our couple-hood and to remember the higher purpose of our journey together. By the time we part each evening, we are more aware of the lessons of unconditional love, more understanding of our "growing pains," and more appreciative of the gift we have been given to serve life together — the creative act of being in a relationship.

Frequently, the evening does not start out that way. The everyday realities of marriage, family, or work can easily overwhelm us. We let our ideals become buried under a pile of practical details and so-called responsibilities. We easily forget that we have only one duty, one responsibility in life: *to love...and love completely.*

Sometimes there are crises; a couple experiencing real difficulty, blocked in their love for each other and yet coming for help. Not long ago a couple came to our group in this condition. We feel they were helped as soon as they walked in our front door, for it takes great courage to admit the need for help. Most couples in disharmony are too proud to reveal their weaknesses. It is safer to stay home and sulk. Sometimes, of course, it is more important to work things out alone, or as a couple. But there are many times when tremendous healing is available through the energy of a like-minded and cohesive group, with understanding that can reach a deeper causative level.

Since every relationship needs ongoing healing, a central purpose of a couple's group is the continual acknowledgement of this, and an asking for help.

As food is necessary for the body, prayer is necessary for the soul...No act of mine is done without prayer...I am not a man of learning, but I humbly claim to be a man of prayer.

MAHATMA GANDHI

Those in a relationship are not an island unto themselves. For the relationship to expand and truly flower, there must be inspiration from other than just the two personalities involved. We need to accept the fact that we need ongoing help, guidance, and support. The support from other spiritually-minded couples is of great value, but even more important is the seeking help and strength from our inner spiritual source.

When we first fall in love there is a great deal of magic, light and joy. It is as if there was a cup between us of living water from which we were drinking, and becoming higher and higher from being together as we drink. At this point we may make the mistake of feeling this is our love, or this is our water to drink, and the supply will never run out. But the water is a gift from the One who watches over us, and is but a sample of so much more. It must be used wisely, and must be replenished from the Source from which it comes. The supply is unlimited, but we must humbly seek it from time to time, and wait to receive...to have the cup filled once again so that we may continue to drink together and grow in love. If the cup is not replenished, there is the risk of it becoming dry,

and then we wonder where the magic and spark of love went.

The ways of replenishing the cup are many, as the paths to God are many. The important thing is that it is done often enough to keep the love relationship alive. As the water level in the cup becomes lower and lower, our desire to work on filling it becomes less and less. When the cup is kept almost full, there is great joy in filling it even more.

When a couple is following a similar spiritual path, it may not be too difficult to find a practice they can both do together, such as meditating and praying together. The hard part may be in disciplining themselves to do it. For those couples who are on different paths, it may take a certain degree of cooperation and creativity to meet on a similar ground. If the intention is there, a way can always be found. I once saw a couple who seemed to be having a great deal of trouble finding a common meeting ground upon which to receive spiritual help. The man was very opposed to all spiritual practices, the woman very much into them. Finally they realized that they each shared a love of nature and plants. They found they could stand together each evening and bless their garden, and ask that their lives together be blessed and that their love flourish like their garden. The couple grew very close in this way, which for them was a source of inspiration.

The ways are many. The important factor is that the couple come together in child-like faith and seek from the one central Source, and then receive into their cup the water, the magic, the spark of love that will keep them united and growing.

Any form of religion is the best form.

NEEM KAROLI BABA (MAHARAJJI)

Do something about doing something.

PEARL DORRIS

Conscious Communication

Said Mrs. Browning, the poet, to Charles Kingsley, the novelist, ''What is the secret of your life? Tell me, that I may make mine beautiful also.'' Thinking a moment, the beloved old author replied, ''I had a friend.''

Honest communication has two main aspects, both equally important. The first has to do with the "honest" part. Is what you have to say not only the truth, but also worth saying? Being an honest chatter-box is not much better than being a regular chatter-box. If we would only learn to take the time to feel before speaking, our communication would replenish rather than tire us out.

The second aspect of honest communication has to do with timing and the receptivity of the listener. This is a very important issue for most of us. For no matter how profound your discourse may be, if the timing or receptivity are not right, you've blown it. This is equally true whether you're telling someone what you don't like about them, or whether you're expounding on their heavenly attributes.

Basically, this is all a matter of getting outside of yourself enough to see, and hear, and feel what is right, and to be sensitive to the other person's needs. If you're all wrapped up in what you have to say, you're not respecting your friend.

Every couple we know struggles with this issue daily. It brings to mind a classic goof I once made. Sometime ago, while our first daughter Rami was just a baby, I was meditating (it was my turn) in our bedroom, while Joyce was changing diapers in the bathroom. It was one of those rare, truly exquisite meditations. I was lifted to a very high state, but by the time I had made my way into the bathroom I was no longer in that state. It was already a memory. Combine that with a somewhat swollen ego, proud of such an accomplishment, and look out!

Joyce, meanwhile, was struggling to change a fussy baby's diapers, and was eagerly awaiting Barry the helper, rather than Barry the guru. When Barry the guru arrived, eyes ablaze, starting to share his mystical experience, he almost got hit in the face with a soiled diaper. It was a classic case of insensitivity and poor timing.

You see, some of this has to do with impulsiveness. We become used to instant gratification, in this case the need to say something. But as we desire oneness...as we desire unconditional love...we learn to listen to more subtle rules of communication. It takes practice, but if you take time to develop your intuitive feelings of the situation, you will be guided in what and when to communicate. If it's something important that must be said, consider first asking inwardly from your heart for help...asking God in you to take command of your voice. Then you will be given the assistance needed.

The communication of a couple goes through a natural process of evolution as their love and commitment grows. In the first or preawakening period, or the early stages of awakening, there is not yet the commitment to truth. There is dishonesty, games, and much hiding. Secondly, as the individuals start on the path of consciousness, of spiritual advancement, often there is a fanatical adherence to total honesty in every way. While the deeper motive is good, there is an impulsiveness to share every thought and feeling, i.e., mistaking honesty for truth. Many get caught in this stage, especially those with psychological training or tendencies. Once, when Joyce and I were stuck in this stage, a beloved teacher told us that this kind of honesty is a burden to the other person. He used the following classic example: When a married couple walk down the street, and an attractive, scantily-clad young woman passes by, the man might have a certain thought or two. If he shared every detail with his wife, can you see how it could be an unnecessary burden on her?

Therefore, in the third stage of communication, we acquire the wisdom to distinguish honesty from truth, and we learn timing. We realize that the highest purpose of communication is communing, which is becoming one with each other. At this point, when we speak, it is the voice of love coming through us with the sole purpose of creating more love. And sometimes our silence may express this even more perfectly.

Barry and I were once counseling a certain couple individually, i.e. the woman came to see me, the man to Barry. In one session with the woman, it seemed nothing was happening. We were talking about issues, yet something was blocking the flow. Finally I asked her to just look at me, and we sat for a long time silently looking into each other's eyes. I asked her if there was something else she needed to share, as it seemed there was a closed door between us. She said she couldn't think of anything. I pushed a bit more, and she burst into tears and told me of an affair she had had one week ago. She was so ashamed of it that she vowed to never tell anyone, including her husband. As she spoke, the door between us opened and the flow of truth brought pain but also life back into her eyes. We talked a long time about the need for truth in her relationship with her husband. Before she left that day, we prayed together for strength and the courage to be truthful. Out of fear, however, she was never able to tell her husband.

Several weeks later, the husband confided in Barry that there seemed to be something preventing him from getting close to his wife. They would reach a certain point in their communication and then they felt blocked and could go no further. As the weeks passed, the wife continued to hold onto her secret and their communication grew worse. Then the husband suddenly became obsessed with thoughts of wanting an affair. Though he had no idea of his wife's one-time involvement with another man, and previously had no desire for this, still he was unconsciously sensitive to her thoughts and was letting them affect his feelings. The couple found themselves wanting to spend less and less time together and they began to drift apart.

Truth is the rock upon which a good relationship is built. With truth comes trust, and upon this foundation a deep and lasting love can be built. If one holds back a vital truth out of fear, or guilt, this will cause the foundation to begin to crumble, and the weeds of doubt and mistrust may begin to take over. Truth can be very hot and may burn as it goes along its path. I know this very deeply in my own marriage. Yet truth can also be the force which purifies and illumines, bringing about a great light. One needs courage and strength to hold to truth, and these are gifts which are freely given if we but ask.

Truth is God.

MAHATMA GANDHI

The imperative thing in the world today is absolute honesty in regard to life. People everywhere think that they are fooling life, but that is not possible. Life cannot be fooled...As you value your progress, be honest with life.

SAINT GERMAIN

PRACTICE

As in the other practices, the preliminary centering is very important to the depth of the experience.

Sit facing each other with eyes closed and relax. Start breathing slowly and deeply. On the in-breath, draw into yourself God's Light and Presence. Feel yourself actually fill to overflowing. Then, on the out-breath, do two things. First, breathe out all your tensions, thoughts, and negativity. Try to get the feeling of how the infilling of love leaves no room for anything else but love.

Second, because love is ever fluid and moving, breathe out this love as your unique gift to life. You breathe in this pure essence, it circulates through your being, taking on your very specific qualities, and then is breathed out to help the world in your own very special way.

Now turn your attention to your life, your unfolding process, both as an individual and as a couple. Let yourself see and/or feel what is your biggest stumbling-block to this unfolding. Specifically, focus on what it is *in you* that is keeping you separated from your beloved. Whatever visual image, feeling or thought passing through your consciousness is valuable in this exercise. Go after the one with the greatest charge of energy, perhaps the one that you would least like to share with your partner. Know that by sharing something difficult about ourselves, we are humbling our personalities before God, our Higher Self. Deep learning takes place with opening, and real opening always involves risk. If we share what we share, and feel we are not risking something, then we are not opening.

The person who risks nothing, does nothing, has nothing, is nothing, and becomes nothing. He may avoid suffering and sorrow, but he simply cannot learn and feel and change and grow and love and live. He's forfeited his freedom. Only the person who risks is truly free.

ANONYMOUS

Now as you get ready to share what you have decided upon, feel how you can do this in two ways. One way has the feeling of keeping the two of you at a distance, of working against each other. This is the way of comfortable intellectualizing or abstractions. The other way uses heartfelt words to work together. It is the way of merging, of communication, of communion.

When you are ready, open your eyes and take turns verbally sharing and risking, and then quietly listening, receiving into your open heart what is shared with you.

Listen, or thy tongue will keep thee deaf.

AMERICAN INDIAN

Separation Into Oneness

...But let there be spaces in your togetherness, And let the winds of the heavens dance between you.
...Sing and dance together and be joyous, but let each one of you be alone. Even as the strings of a lute are alone though they quiver with the same music.

KAHLIL GIBRAN

Having space from each other is very important in a relationship. What is even more important is how this time is used. If the couple is having problems and each chooses to go off seeking distractions or another partner, this will obviously hinder them from growing closer, for one purpose of time apart should be to draw the couple closer together in spirit, as well as to draw us into greater appreciation of our own soul.

Once, we saw a couple who had been traveling across the U.S. They had met one year previously and had felt a very high, intense contact and commitment to each other. Each was very interested in working on themselves and coming to God. Each felt the other was the perfect balance and that, if they could be together every minute, all of their unclear areas would come up to be dealt with and then be burned away. They embarked on a year's pilgrimage in which they were to be together every minute.

By the time we met with them one year later, they could hardly stand each other. There had been no space. It had gotten serious and had stayed that way. Sometimes only the gentle rain of one's tears in solitude can wash clear a space and bring renewed love. Many negative areas had come up for this couple but, because of the lack of space, they had gotten burned, so to speak, in their own fire.

Right now, Barry and I have two small girls. As any parent of small children knows, there is much to be done. We spend time together, but much of it is caring for the girls. If I don't watch it, I find myself seeing Barry more in terms of my helper with the children, than as my lover, friend, and spiritual partner. Then my thoughts go somewhat like, "Barry can change Mira's diapers, or he can read Rami her story, or I wish he would do more for them." When my thoughts run only like that in relation to Barry, then I know I'm off-center, and need time alone.

In my aloneness, I do a practice that we recommend for all

couples. I pray to feel Barry's presence, to experience his soul — who he really is. I sit with my eyes closed and picture him before me at a time when we have felt a special closeness with each other. Then one by one I draw my attention to the beautiful qualities of his inner being, such as his gentleness, sensitivity, and his deep love for God. Sometimes it takes a little work but, if done with persistence, I feel wrapped in God's love coming through Barry. He again becomes my beloved. Then I pray for the strength to hold that feeling of who he really is.

When I return to the family, many times nothing will have changed outwardly with them, and it may have become even busier in my absence. But I have changed and can look over at Barry and feel the depth of our love. He feels it right away, as do the girls, and we are all happier. Sometimes, I feel that in my aloneness I give the most to Barry. By concentrating on his inner beauty (those divine qualities present in all of us), I am not only allowing space in our relationship, but also drawing those qualities out of us both.

We have to be mindful (and heartful) of the cycles of our relationships, and especially our own individual cycles and needs. So many arguments and other problems are due to ignoring, or perhaps not respecting, either your own or your partner's need for space, quiet, or aloneness. Actually, it is most important to respect your own needs, for that will give you the sensitivity to the needs of those around you.

There perhaps can be no more important aspect of a living relationship than the right use of solitude. Someday, we'll all be firmly rooted in the center of our being, unaffected by the ego of our partner — or our own ego. But right now there is a delicate balance between time together and time apart. Too much of one or the other will throw the relationship out of balance.

Too much time spent together is one side of the coin. In this case the sensitivity and respect for one another can be easily lost. The relationship can become dulled, or else it can become very serious from too much "working it out," as in the couple Joyce mentioned. There is also a subtle fear of loneliness or aloneness ("all-one-ness") which causes couples to cling to one another. This fear must be overcome to keep the relationship breathing.

The other side of the coin is too much time spent apart. Often this is an offshoot of too much time together. The relationship may have gotten too hot, too intense, and one or both partners find more and more excuses to be away from home. I remember the months after our first daughter, Rami's, birth. It was a time of incredible closeness and growth for Joyce and me. Our house was literally charged with the intensity of the vibrations. So much so, however, that I found myself getting more and more involved in activities away from the house. I was amazed at how many opportunities arose for me to be away from home. Then one day I woke up to what was happening — that I was running away, not from Joyce or Rami, but from myself. It was too much for me.

Too much personal contact can get scary, like looking too long or too close in a mirror. Parts of ourselves are exposed in our reflection in our lover's eyes — parts that we never knew existed, or are not ready to admit to. It's so easy to get lost in the projection: "It's you, not me!"

Our relationships could have so much more beauty, so much more wonder, if we only made better use of our time apart (as well as our time together). The art of separation is either not appreciated, or not sufficiently cultivated. Most final separations could have been prevented with the right use of little separations. For in our times apart, we sometimes have the greatest opportunity to develop our relationship. It's what makes the difference between those two old sayings: "Absence makes the heart grow fonder" and "Out of sight, out of mind." We are constantly, although more or less consciously, choosing between these two. The one quickens love, the other kills our relationship.

Maybe it's laziness as much as fear that causes so many of us to stop working to renew love. We find someone else to be with who doesn't seem to push any of our sensitive buttons (yet). It's easier, or we feel loved and appreciated without our having to work at it. However, we ultimately realize that true love comes only through overcoming barriers and passing the tests given to us by life. And the greatest barrier and test is our own mind.

Once, before Mira's birth, Joyce and Rami traveled to Buffalo, New York, for a visit with her parents. I realized it was an opportunity to have 10 days alone for a retreat, as well as a chance to deepen our relationship.

No sooner had they left than I plummeted into a whirlwind of activity, filling the first several days with finishing projects around the house. I was in the middle of two or three different activities when this tiny thought crept into my mind: "Barry, you're failing your test." Aha! It was "out of sight, out of mind." I sat right down, closed my eyes, and asked God for help in quieting my mind and opening my heart. I did the practice Joyce suggested. I visualized her in the highest moment of our life together. I remembered the scene. She was almost luminous with ecstasy. She was like a master, pouring her love into me. She was the Mother giving birth to me, and I could feel my heart yet once again being born, stirring within me with new life, with a deep yearning for my beloved.

Be able to be alone. Lose not the advantage of solitude...but delight to be alone and single with Omnipresency...Life is a pure flame, and we live by an invisible sun within us.

SIR THOMAS BROWN (1605-1682)

PRACTICE

An important, and yet often neglected, means of deepening the peace in the love relationship is the practice of periods of silence. We have often done this, and it has always brought greater harmony into our relationship.

We suggest you set aside any agreed-upon time period, such as an evening. Start out small, for being over-ambitious and setting too large an amount of time can have a reverse effect, creating more tension than harmony.

Spend the time period together in a loving way, rather than avoiding each other — and OBSERVE SILENCE. If you want (or need) to communicate, do it in writing, and ideally, keep it to a minimum.

This practice teaches us how much time and energy we waste in idle chatter. Silence is truly "golden." It opens the door for communication with our whole being, rather than our mind alone.

Then, after resuming oral communication, feel how your consciousness has been "sharpened." Now try to make every sentence meaningful — an expression of your whole being.

Eye Contact Work

On looking at what is in the mirror in front of you, think of what is behind it.

WU WANG

One of the fastest ways to increase the depth and clarity of a relationship is working with eye contact. In our individual work with couples and in our classes, we often have people face each other and allow them time to look deeply into one another's eyes. Many people rarely, if ever, take time to do this. Many are afraid of what they'll see in the mirror of projection, or they may be afraid of letting go and entering real intimacy.

People who are new at this sometimes burst into laughter as a result of the intensity of the energy. This kind of working together is very powerful. To be effective, and a vehicle for spiritual growth, it requires patience, self-control, and more patience. The laughter is due to a heightened awareness of body and personality...or just plain old-fashioned embarrassment.

As you let go and relax, you may be privileged (with the grace of God) to experience seeing through the "veils," where you sit in love looking upon the beloved. Usually, people are given a glimpse of this quite early in this exercise. To me it feels like a gift, and also a taste, to whet our appetites for what lies ahead of us all in our lives.

Sometimes, it seems as if a door then closes on the experience. What really happened is that you started to think about what you were experiencing, rather than just experiencing. Actually, you closed the door. But there is no need to get down on yourself, for something else is happening on quite another level. That moment of heightened (or better, expanded) awareness triggers a natural process. When the Light increases, even momentarily, it also penetrates into those darkened corners of our whole being, into subconscious areas that we wish we didn't have. These "boogie" aspects of our personality can be brought to the surface very quickly in an exercise like this or in any conscious work on yourself. This is the "shadow" that Jung described so well. These are the elements lurking in the closets of your ego that destroy your good intentions, sabotage your well-meaning plans, and seek to pull you down like gravity force, into a pit.

All of this can happen very fast. One minute your whole being wells up with love and delight, with wonderful lightness in your body...and correspondingly, the face in front of you is radiantly beautiful. The next minute it's gone, and some not so pleasant things are happening. Strange sensations may pull you, and very often the face in front of you may reflect everything you're going through, sometimes alarmingly so. As the ancient teachings say, "You see what you are."

You may perhaps want to do this kind of work with a special friend, and again find you're thrown right into this latter experience. Any experience you have is revealing what work *you* need to do! Not your partner! It is *so* easy to smugly sit there and observe, or even analyze your wife's (or husband's) neurosis. How often have I done that! Be courageous! Admit to yourself that you're looking into the mirror, *that everything you see out there is at this moment reflecting the state you're in.* Projection can be your worst enemy in life; breeding fear, anger, hate, and much more, or it can be a very great experience for expanding self-knowledge. And self-knowledge without criticism leads to God-knowledge. For true "know-ledge" is jumping over the "ledge" of the "knowing" of the finite mind.

Herein lies the next step. It is not enough to merely acknowledge the mirror of life, and then get on your own case for all your faults, wallowing in self-pity or self-contempt. Now you need to ask within yourself for help to let go of all judgments. Tune into that vast power in your heart, which flows through you at all times. This is the great test of your life. It is the alchemical changing of base metals into gold. It cannot be done with your mind alone. When your feet become planted on the real path, the Way, you see how helpless your mind is by itself, how pride in your own abilities is preventing your growth. Pray for help, ask for help, and you'll get it. It comes from within.

Gratitude is perhaps the fastest way to grow. Whenever you can let go enough to thank the universe for a certain problem, you become the solution to that problem. For "solution" literally means becoming liquid enough to dissolve the particles making up the problem. True gratitude will always do that.

PRACTICE

Sit together facing your partner. Close your eyes and do your own work of coming into the moment...relax, breathe, affirm, pray, whatever you do to center.

Then, when ready, open your eyes and look at your partner. It's not enough to merely look. Try to allow yourself to see and be seen. Allow yourself to be open. Overcome the tendency to get too outside of yourself. Always keep in touch with your own process...sensations in your body, thoughts and feelings.

Relax even more. Body loose. Breathing deep, slow, and rhythmic. Can you see something in the face in front of you strangely familiar...kind of like a friend behind the friend. Most of the time you see one person, but now catch a glimpse of the deeper person. Can you recognize the one before you? Your friendship goes back much farther than you think...much farther than you can ever imagine. This face has a definite ancient appearance to it...in fact, timeless. And at the same time it is the face of a child, with all the wonder and sparkle of youth. Yes, both simultaneously! The face is neither masculine nor feminine, but in a strange way is both. Go ahead, look! This is your lover. Can you feel that attraction beyond description? Can you see that rare beauty so refined that you feel it is a sacred honor just to sit here before this one? This is your teacher. Can you feel how protected and guided you are...that you are loved with a love beyond love? This is your child...open, trusting completely as you mold his or her life with your slightest thought. This is your friend....your very life is a sacred trust to him or her. You are now not just looking without, but also within. For in truth, this is God, the Eternal Being. *And God can only see God.* So behold the beauty of your being.

Now close your eyes and ask, with all the sincerity of your being, to be allowed to remember who you are in the course of your daily lives together.

eleven

Getting Straight With Our Parents

Honor thy Father and thy Mother

OLD TESTAMENT

I am in all relationships as a thread through a string of pearls.

There comes a point in our spiritual journey when we discover that we cannot progress until we have cleared negativity from our relationship with our parents. We need to feel love, forgiveness and respect for our physical parents, or we will be held back from achieving true closeness with our partner and others. This does not mean that we must spend every weekend with our parents, or have them move in, or even be with them at all (as is the case of a parent who has passed on). But it does mean our thoughts toward them need to become ever more loving, forgiving, and filled with gratitude for who they are. As this gradually happens, the door to our heart will open ever wider and we will also be able to love all others more fully.

For those of us following the path of consciousness, it is not beneficial to look back upon our childhood and blame our parents for the weaknesses we have, or for the negative conditions in our lives. We need to be open to the possibility that, as relatively conscious souls, we looked around and chose our parents before incarnating upon the earth. Sometimes the greatest weakness in a parent is the quality we were needing most to overcome a weakness in our own being. Also, what we may see as a parent's greatest weakness may in fact be covering up a great strength.

Once while working with a group of women, we each focused on our relationship with our parents. I asked the women to pick out the most beautiful quality in the parent they felt the most removed from. (Try this for yourselves right now). One woman especially cringed. After some gentle pushing, she revealed that her father had been an alcoholic her entire life, and had caused the family much suffering. She could never remember him as the warm, fatherly type she would have wanted. As the group worked together and prayed to see beauty in this parent, the woman suddenly burst into tears. She then related a story that had completely escaped her memory.

Once, as a small child, her father had come home from his first job as a forest ranger. There had been a forest fire and he had helped fight it. He sat the girl on his knee and told her how he had seen burned and frightened animals running through the forest ablaze with fire. He had then cried bitterly at the thought of the animals' suffering. In recalling the memory, she realized how very sensitive her father was to the sufferings of others, and how he had turned to alcohol as an escape. She realized that beautiful quality of sensitivity he had and how she shared that with him. Moreover, she was attracted to and married a man who, like her father, was very sensitive and receptive and sometimes tried to cover that up. When the woman finished relating her story, she felt not only love and forgiveness for her father, but also an increased love for her husband, and greater appreciation for who he was.

It's also good to remember that we may have been difficult for our parents to raise. We may have incarnated with a different level of consciousness than our parents. It might have been a real shock for them to witness certain aspects of our being coming to the surface. Barry, who is now a vegetarian with a great respect for the animal kingdom, was born into a Jewish family from New York. Imagine their dismay when he had a strong aversion to meat: "My son doesn't like meat, he'll starve!!" It was a shock, and he was taken to many a doctor to find out what was wrong, and there was much conflict at mealtime. If we can look with humor upon what our parents may have gone through, we will have much more compassion for them.

I remember a stage of growth Joyce and I went through in the early 70's. At that time, we were deeply impressed by the need to "get straight" with our parents, ie. to bring those relationships into a higher awareness. We were seeing with alarming clarity to what extent our own marriage relationship was a direct reflection of the patterns we had fallen into with our parents. We concluded that if we could be totally honest with our parents, it would free us all. Our motives were inherently good, but our immaturity and impulsiveness caused much unnecessary suffering on all sides. We would have marathon encounter sessions with our parents. As you can imagine, it made them very uncomfortable. Our level of "honesty" was not truth. Rather than being sensitive of their space, we were mostly burdening them with our ideas of what should be, or how we should relate. What we were doing was simply continuing our adolescent stuggle for independence, but on another level. It was a hard lesson, but we learned.

True independence is an inner state, and has nothing to do with what is said or done outwardly. It is the gradual emergence of grateful and respectful feelings for who our parents are — not how well they have played their roles. Here I am thirty-seven years old, and when my parents come for a visit, my mother hugs me, looks at me, and sometimes even talks to me as if I'm still seven years old. I can see that it will probably be the same when I'm fifty. But it doesn't seem to matter anymore, because I feel the love of *the* Mother behind my mother. The love is there, but it comes out in the form that she knows best. I used to angrily say, "Mom, I'm not your little boy anymore!" Now I eat it up. It's freeing to enjoy being a little boy in my mother's eyes. After all, I am that too!

As this has happened with my mother, there has been a direct correlation with my marriage. I'm still quite capable of being a stubborn and rebellious little rascal, but I'm also learning to surrender to the love of the Mother as it comes through Joyce, even in ways that are strange to me. I can more and more enjoy being mothered…even s-mothered…as I feel Who it really is who is loving me.

A man once came to me for counseling. His initial complaint was marital difficulties, but it soon became clear that the real issue was his relationship with his father. This may seem strange at first, but when one human relationship is problematic, there is a carryover to all other relationships. This man's heart was closed to his father, so he could not fully open to his wife, or to anyone else.

As a little boy, this man had worshipped his father as most little boys do. Then, entering the years of late childhood and adolescence, a disenchantment set in. He saw his father as weak, self-centered, and ignorant. He no longer respected him and grew to despise him as well. All communication broke down. At the age of eighteen he went away to college, and had not lived at home since. He learned to adapt himself to a superficial relationship with his father which prevailed whenever he visited.

Later during marriage his aloofness and distancing techniques finally manifested into the present crisis. A pending separation had caused him to seek counseling. Feeling the connection between his marital difficulties and his relationship with his father, I asked him to share his father's strengths with me. He told me his father had none. I insisted, sharing how I felt his marriage depended on it…that he needed to go beyond the stubborness and rebelliousness he was projecting onto me as well as his father. That shook him a bit. He started by revealing some of his father's minor positive qualities, such as providing an income, being responsible, honest, and so on. This gave momentum to the process, however, which allowed him to go deeper. He began to see that although his father lacked education and verbal ability, he was a feeling-oriented man with a deep sensitivity who understood and related to the world in that way. Suddenly, eyes brimming with tears, he saw how lonely his father was, and how much pain he had to endure.

Not long afterwards, this man had the opportunity to visit his parents. Remembering the session, he tried to be warmer toward his father, but years of habit patterns seemed to interfere. Finally he gave up and went out to visit friends. When he returned home late that night, he was surprised to see his father sitting all alone reading. A strange sensation seemed to pull him toward his father. Yielding to this, he went over and sat next to him. The older man started talking, a little about the book, but more just to make conversation. The young man listened, but he began to look at his father. For the first time in his life, he saw this man not as his father, but as a human being with joys and pains, happiness as well as sadness, victory as well as failure. He saw a man who loved him deeply but did not know how to show it. His father continued talking, but now the son was exploring new feelings. A great love was welling up in his heart for this unsophisticated, simple, and beautiful old man.

The father noticed the moist brightness in his son's eyes and stopped talking. He fumbled over a few more words, then stopped again.

"I love you, dad." The son was surprised at the strength and courage in his words.

"I love you too, son." Now the old man's eyes were moist too.

The young man leaned over and embraced his father. They sat there in silence while a healing took place between two souls.

All was different from that time on. One weak link in a large chain of love was strengthened, and therefore the whole chain was strengthened. A new warmth entered his relationships: with his wife, with me, with everyone.

When a man sees beauty in his father, he heals their relationship. When he can experience his father as another child of God like himself, he then becomes a wider channel for the father-aspect of God — the Father Presence within himself. His heart can then open to all men and, through this, to all humanity.

There is a group of men I meet with, all of whom are working with these issues. We come together with the sole purpose of opening our hearts to one another and to God, and breaking down the age-old barriers that prevent men from truly loving one another. Men in our culture are conditioned to relate to each other on a mental level that is devoid of warmth and feeling. In the group we hug each other, share our deepest joys and sorrows, and learn to feel the essence of our manhood. By doing this we also learn something about our fatherhood. For the feeling of father is man made whole, i.e. the fulfillment of man. We then love each other in the way a good father loves his children, not as a superior, but as an equal with no strings attached. When we touch this, we not only can love our human father, we can also love our Heavenly Father, the father-aspect of God. Indeed, we have become one with the Father. We *are* the Father-God loving all His children.

I once saw a woman in counseling who had been married four years. She and her husband were both counselors, and the woman in particular had very keen sensitivity into other people. She was beginning to experience difficulty in the relationship with her husband, though, and intuitively felt it had something to do with her relationship with her mother. She didn't like her mother and had moved 3,000 miles away hoping to never see her again. Now six years later she was beginning to sense that this block in loving her mother was affecting all her relationships, especially her marriage.

I asked what her mother had done that was so wrong and she gave me a whole list of offenses. At the top of the list was her mother's difficulty in controlling her anger. She would yell, scream, slam doors and cry alot. The anger was often directed at her daughter with the intention of hurting her. As we talked further the woman realized that as an adolescent her intuitive nature had been highly developed, allowing her to read into other people's lives. She began pointing out her mother's flaws and weaknesses with much accuracy, but also with a feeling of superiority and scorn. Her mother naturally became angry, and in turn, used whatever means she could to put her daughter down. This pattern continued for years. Through talking, the woman realized how she had really been at fault. She was the one who had misused her highly-developed sense of insight against her mother, who was really a very simple person. She then realized how the same pattern had started with her husband, who was the more emotional of the two. She had much to learn from the emotional natures of both her husband and her mother.

After these realizations, the woman welled up with love for her mother. She then felt compassion for the strength her mother must have needed to raise her. As she felt love and forgiveness for her own mother, she could begin to feel and accept the mother-feeling within herself. As this happened, she was able to feel more love for her husband, and see the ways she could help rather than hinder him.

We need to remember that, while growing up, our qualities might have emerged with great force and determination. Our parents may not have known how to handle us.

Another woman related a story to me of how her mother would come to her with great frustration, and complain that none of her friend's daughters had turned out the way she did. The woman at first took this as a direct rejection and felt very hurt. However, it was true, she was different. The awakening process had started very early in her life and she realized a deep affinity with the Eastern religions. While her peers were properly going to church and marrying respectable men, she preferred to meditate, chant mantras and travel on spiritual quests.

As the woman grew in understanding she realized, of course, her mother wasn't rejecting her. Instead, she was feeling guilty of failing her daughter in some way. She had always tried to give her daughter a strong spiritual background in the Christian faith. When her daughter turned to other means for her awakening process, she felt a keen sense of failure. This took the form of disapproval, which saddened both of them. My friend further realized that her mother had not failed in the least. She had instilled such a love of God in her heart that her thirst was unquenchable, and she had turned to the study of all religions. When she was able to humbly communicate that understanding to her mother, they both grew quite close.

There comes a time in our relationship with our parents when

we must stop seeking their approval and begin to approve of them. Chances are, if we haven't received our parents' approval by adulthood...that is, what we think we want from them...we may never receive it. Some people spend their entire lives trying every means they can think of to gain their parents' approval, and end up very frustrated. Our concentration needs to be changed from wanting to receive love, to looking for ways to give love. This simple act can have great impact on our relationships, especially with our mates.

For example, a woman once came to see me complaining that her husband never said anything nice to her. He was quick to criticize and seemed to never appreciate her. She went out of her way to please him by cooking the foods he liked, dressing the way he liked, and doing the things he wanted her to do. She did little for herself. Finally she felt terribly upset by the situation and wanted to leave him. The conversation soon swung around to her relationship with her father. It seemed that her father never approved of her, even though she tried very hard to win his favor. She would go out of her way to please him and, when he didn't comment, she would feel rejected. She later married and started the same pattern with her husband. She would do something special for him, then wait for his approval. When it didn't come right away, she would attack him for his lack of approval.

She and I then focused on the need to seek ways of approving, rather than seeking approval. We receive appreciation by appreciating others. I suggested she feel all the beautiful aspects of her father and find a way to express her appreciation of him; then at home, to concentrate on ways of approving of her husband, rather than being so sensitive and judgmental regarding his lack of approval.

I saw the woman several years later. She and her husband were much happier together. She told me she had written to her father, expressing great appreciation for who he was. The very act of sending the letter had a freeing effect on her, and she was then able to concentrate on appreciating her husband. The husband in turn picked up on the change in his wife, and began to notice and appreciate her more.

There had also been a subtle change with her father. In his usual manner he had made no comment about the letter he received from her, but whenever they were together he seemed much happier. Finally the woman asked him if he had received the letter, and rather embarrassed he replied, "Yes I did."

Years later the woman had a chance to look into her father's treasure drawer. This was a little drawer in which he saved the most treasured items of his life. In it she saw all of her baby teeth, his college ring, his mother's wedding band, and yes, that letter of appreciation from his daughter.

It is also possible to heal a relationship with a parent who has passed on, even many years ago. Once, a sensitive, beautiful man came for counseling because he was having trouble staying in a relationship with a woman. He was very aware of his feelings, and related his difficulty to his mother's death twenty years ago, when he was nine years old. He still carried a slight feeling of anger and resentment toward his mother, that she had left him when he needed her the most.

Now, whenever he would reach a point of need or attachment with a woman, he would be afraid that she, like his mother, would leave him. Out of this fear of being similarly hurt, he would end the relationship. As aware as he was of his feelings, he seemed unable to break this pattern.

In our session together, I asked him to close his eyes and convey as much of his mother's death as he could remember. He described the funeral service and his feelings of sorrow as he saw his beloved mother's body in the coffin. He remembered everyone crying and saying what a great loss it was now that she was gone. He remembered how relatives, in an attempt to comfort him, told him his mother was now in heaven. The feeling they conveyed to him, however, was of permanent loss.

Through the use of guided meditation I asked him to remember his feelings the first night after his mother's death as he lay alone in bed. Suddenly he started crying and said, "I felt my mother's comforting hand upon my head, soothing me as I drifted to sleep." Through deep sobs he remembered how he had experienced this same feeling each night upon going to sleep, an experience of his mother's continued love for him.

Then he remembered his grief-stricken father deciding to remarry after three months to ease the deep pain he felt. He told his son that from now on he was to have a new mother. The man remembered how he had protested the idea of a new mother, and told his father of the nightly visits he was having with his own mother. The father, probably feeling guilty about remarrying so soon, impatiently told the son those visits were nonsense — his mother was gone to heaven and could never come back. The man cried very deeply as he remembered how he did not allow himself to experience his mother's loving presence after that time, and how he had gradually closed his heart to her.

As a result of his realization in the session, he then opened to her presence in his life and once again felt the loving hand of his mother soothing him. He realized she had never gone anywhere. He was the one who had closed the door to their relationship. He knew in that moment that he need never fear the loss of love as long as he kept the door of his heart open.

I have not seen this man again. But I feel quite certain that by opening to his mother's ever-present love, he will deepen all his relationships.

When we heal our relationship with our parents, we are healing a deep part of ourselves, and this will enhance all our relationships. The most beautiful changes in our lives will be the ever-deepening ability to love the Father-Mother God. For our physical mother is the first channel for the Divine Mother. To close our heart to her is to block the flow of the Divine Mother's love to us. Our physical father, or father-figure, is the first channel for the Heavenly Father. To be in deeper communion with Him, we must be able to love our own physical father. Likewise, loving our physical mother and father helps to then love and accept the mother and father within us all. Once united within, we can then reach out to love, serve, and bless many.

Honor thy Earthly Mother, that thy days may be long upon the land, and honor thy Heavenly Father, that eternal life be thine in the heavens . . .

FROM THE ESSENE TEN COMMANDMENTS

twelve

Thoughts on Abortion

Learn that eternity is now, the future is now. There is no past or present or future as separate periods of time — all is within the soul's embrace now. It is the reaction to the now which is your future. Never look into the future and anticipate this, that, or the other, for to do so is to live in fear. Live today with God, and your future can hold nothing but joy.

WHITE EAGLE

It is difficult to write about abortion. Few of us here on earth really know the spiritual consequences. People's feelings about abortion range from first degree murder to merely a form of birth control. In the merging process of a couple, this question sometimes arises and is a decision for both partners. I have never had an abortion myself, but I have gone through the experience with many different couples and single women in the course of our counseling experience. I offer their stories as illustrations of ways people have worked with this complex issue.

The first couple was in their thirties. They were unmarried and living together with the hope of soon marrying. They loved one another very much, but they did have some difficulties in relating, which at times threatened to overwhelm their commitment. Barry and I had seen them intermittently in counseling and they seemed to be growing closer all the time. We saw them at an annual Christmas gathering where they radiated a great degree of love and happiness. They told us that in the last month they had felt so much love for each other that some of the negative attitudes toward each other were vanishing.

A very odd thing happened after they left. I began to feel as if I were pregnant. I had no physical symptoms, and yet I felt a soul very close to me. The beauty of this being was so great that I became excited. Two weeks later Barry received a call from the couple that they were six weeks pregnant. He came to tell me and then I knew that the soul I had been feeling so strongly was their child, not mine. I felt so happy for them, as this being had also connected with me and I knew of its great beauty and strength. I felt the couple was indeed very blessed, and that this being was coming as a helper — for them and the world. The vision had come so clearly, so quickly, and had thrilled me with such joy that I was unprepared for what followed.

Barry went on, ''They want to get an abortion right away and want to talk with us.'' It was a challenge for me as I later listened to their reasons for not wanting the child: not feeling ready, not trusting the other to be a good parent, wanting to work more, feeling the child would be in the way of accomplishment in the world, and not wanting to give up the special intimacy between the two of them. I could feel and understand all of their doubts and fears about having this child. Yet from the depths of my heart I knew of the blessing to be chosen as the parents of this child. The couple decided to go through with the abortion. Two years later I again saw the woman. She confided in me that from that day on their relationship had gone down-hill. They were now in a painful process of separating permanently.

From all that I have seen, I believe strongly that children come as a blessing into our lives, although the timing is not always as we would have it, and seemingly there are untold barriers along the way. Our minds are so small in comparison to the infinite plan. Often a great spiritual blessing is rejected because the situation may not seem right at the time. Even so, I believe that God does not punish us for this rejection but continues to try to strengthen us and bring us deeper into Divine Love.

The second story is a little different. A young couple came to us with two small children, ages four and two. They were devoted to the children and were good parents. The woman found herself pregnant for the third time and was most unhappy about the prospects of a third child. She had been nursing for four years and the littlest one had just stopped. She was beginning to taste a new freedom in her life and was enjoying going out by herself. Most mothers can deeply relate to her feelings. The thought of yet another baby to nurse and care for weighed heavily upon her. The husband also was not too excited about the prospects of caring for another child. However, he had already felt the presence of the child in a moment of deep inner peace, and was feeling fatherly feelings. The woman wanted to get an abortion. The man felt that an abortion of this baby would be the same as killing one of the other children, and he was very opposed to it. She felt that since the baby was coming through her body it was her decision, and she went ahead and had the abortion.

The husband went through a very painful process, but in the end supported his wife after the abortion had taken place. The woman experienced a lot of sadness after the abortion, but pushed it aside as best she could. The couple continued to love each other and their two children. However, both reported a feeling of loss, an indescribable sadness that existed in their hearts. Five months later the woman became pregnant again. Again she grew unhappy at the prospect of having a third child. The husband again felt the presence of this child and this time suffered greatly when his wife had a second abortion. The woman similarly suffered again after this abortion. She tried throwing herself into more and more outside activities and classes. Previously she had enjoyed these a great deal, but now they could not mask the feelings of loss. Something was not quite right in her life. The couple started having trouble with their marriage, and wanted to spend less time with each other and the children.

Three months later the unborn child again knocked on their door. The woman was pregnant again. This time she surrendered and invited this being into her life. She had a beautiful pregnancy with this child and during the nine months the family seemed to grow closer in union and harmony. A beautiful baby girl was born and, as she grew she seemed to fill a need in each member of the family, to take away that feeling of loss and give abundant love in its place. The mother especially reported that this child was very special to her. The child's presence in her life was the missing in-gredient she was needing to grow closer to God.

The trouble with abortion is that we just do not realize who it is that we are rejecting. Perhaps this is our dearest spiritual teacher who is coming to bless our life and strengthen us, and we unknow-ingly reject him or her for the sake of convenience. I have spoken with many very sensitive and spiritually-minded women who have had abortions. All have reported a feeling of loss which has sometimes continued for years. I, like most women, know of the inner struggle that exists when my period is late and it seems a pregnancy is coming at a most unwanted time. We know so little of God's plan for our lives. Our minds map out a neat, perfect little road for life and we hate to have it changed in any way. *Yet that perfect little road may completely by-pass our goal of God-realization.* These little beings often serve to bring us right back to where we should be going.

We need faith and surrender when a little one knocks on our heart and body and asks to come inside. It is a faith that knows God is giving us a gift and is giving it with a love and wisdom often hard to comprehend. I have worked in counseling with single women who have chosen to have their baby, despite the lack of support from the father. One woman especially touched my heart and life very deeply. She had conceived her baby with great joy and love. When her man-friend found out she was pregnant, he wanted her to get an abortion right away. He told her he would not support her in any way. She struggled very deeply. She wanted to follow the man's wishes, yet it felt wrong in her heart. With each new day she sensed the unique beauty of the child coming to her and she knew she truly loved this being. She loved the baby's father, yet she could not betray her heart, and decided to keep the baby.

The man left her. He refused to support her throughout the pregnancy or after the baby came. I saw this woman go through in-credible trials in the course of the pregnancy. We talked about how this pregnancy was like a great spiritual fire, burning and transforming her. With each week she became deeper, more courageous, more beautiful, closer to God — despite the hardships of bringing forth the child alone. I was very blessed to attend that birth. The energy when her little boy was born was such that everyone in the room felt a great sacredness in his presence. When I later saw the little boy at eighteen months of age, he was running all around getting into everything, like any little boy his age. Yet there was such a light to his being. It felt like an honor to be around him. The woman has been transformed and now radiates a great strength. It is like she has grown years spiritually, just in the course of bringing forth and raising this child. It has not been easy, yet her inner growth has been beautiful to behold.

Now I want to share a story of a couple who put as much consciousness as they possibly could into their abortion and, in so doing, grew closer. It is rare that we ever do emergency counseling but, when this couple called late one night with their story, we had them come right over. Both the man and woman were twenty-one years of age. They met when they were eighteen and felt a powerful connection and love between them. Six months later they unexpectantly conceived a child. Neither one wanted a child at such an early age but, because of strong religious and family upbringing, each felt that abortion was wrong. They proceeded with the pregnancy and had a beautiful little boy. They stayed together and raised the child as best they could under the circumstances. The man wanted desperately to go to medical school and struggled through college while trying to support his girlfriend and their child. She similarly struggled to complete her education while caring for her baby.

Then she became pregnant with a second child while her first child was not yet two. Though the pregnancy came at a most unwanted time, the woman had made a spiritual link with the soul of the child. The man went into an almost violent rage and insisted she have an abortion immediately. The more he yelled and screamed the more she held fast to the opposite side. He was getting really crazy and threatened to drag her to an abortion counseling center, at which point they called us.

In no time he came stomping into our home yelling at his girlfriend. She huddled in the corner and cried. It was obvious that within the man there was deep pain that was coming out as anger. Barry worked with him for awhile and asked him to get past the anger, to contact his feelings of wanting to abort his child. He sat for a moment, then burst out into deep, deep sobs. He said he felt like a murderer, yet felt he was under so much stress he could not possibly bear anything else. He cried and cried. He confessed to his partner that he too had felt the unborn child in a single moment of peace. That single moment had been enough, for he already loved it. The conflict within him was so great that he just wanted to get an abortion right away, hoping the feeling would go away. As he cried, his girl-friend held him. Now they were united, facing a

hard situation together. Then they left and we watched as they held each other and cried together all the way to their car. They both knew that they would abort this child, but were willing to take an honest look at their feelings.

The woman later told me that they went home that night and prayed together for the first time in their relationship. Previously they had felt far away from God, but on this occasion felt a desperate need for divine, forgiving love. As they prayed, they talked to their unborn child and asked for forgiveness. They both reported a warmth enfolding them. This experience later spurred them into a more spiritual life. The abortion was hard for them both, yet they supported each other fully, despite the feeling of loss and sadness. Shortly afterwards, the couple decided to get married and began praying for that soul to return to them. Because they never stopped loving and wanting that child, two years later their prayers were answered.

Seeking God's forgiveness is so very important. The deepest feeling for most women and men after having an abortion, even for therapeutic reasons, is that they have gone against God's will, that they have erred in God's sight. Many will not report this feeling immediately. One woman told me abortion seemed like just part of birth control to her — a little unpleasant feeling, but necessary. Yet when asked to go further and further still into the depths of her heart there was deep pain. It is at this point that we need to ask for forgiveness. Forgiveness is always there if we but ask. With our hearts fully opened, we must knock and knock upon the door of forgiveness and not stop until it is opened.

A friend of mine called recently and asked for my prayers. She was happily married and a dedicated, loving mother to her four young children. Motherhood had become her path to God and she was a great inspiration to many. However, she was sick for the sixth time in one year. Her illnesses were becoming longer and more intense. Medical doctors could find nothing wrong. After we talked she decided to seek the help of a spiritual healer she had confidence in.

A week later she phoned back happy to report that a great burden had been lifted from her and her health had returned. During the treatment the healer discovered that she had an abortion twenty years ago. She was young at the time and her parents had forced it upon her. She kept her abortion in a dark, secret chamber of her heart and told no one but her husband. As she grew in consciousness over the years, she realized more and more the privilege and honor of motherhood. The abortion consequently seemed uglier and uglier. Unconsciously she had been punishing herself by illness for an act done twenty years ago. The healer exposed all of this and had her pray for forgiveness. She felt her Heavenly Mother's love surround her. The pain and guilt of that abortion melted away. Her health has been fine ever since.

Barry and I have been leading a series of groups entitled "The Healing of the Personality." In one group a woman let go of her guilt that had been smoldering since her abortion over ten years ago. She was working on her inability to deeply love others. Her marriage lasted a short while, leaving her with two children to care for by herself. These children later elected to return to their father, leaving the woman all alone. No relationship seemed to work out for her. She would get to a certain depth with a person, then feel her love run cold.

We were trying different approaches with her but nothing seemed to bring about an emotional release. Finally a strong inner prompting caused me to ask if she had ever had an abortion. She looked at me for a long intense moment. I could tell that she was struggling between an automatic response of "no" and the light of truth which was welling up within her. Finally she burst into tears as she responded "yes"! While she cried, the group members moved very close. We all placed our hands upon her and asked that God's forgiving love be shown. In between sobs she said she had never told anyone about the abortion. Then as her emotional release was at its peak she said, "I've always felt God thought of me as a bad person. I never felt I deserved love." The light, warmth and love was very strong in the room as this woman opened to the healing power of God's grace. We all felt honored to witness such a healing.

We need to know that no matter what may have occurred in our past, it is never too late to turn to God with a sincere heart. Whenever we ask for forgiveness we will receive God's blessing and love and be enfolded in the protecting arms of our Heavenly Parents.

One way to do this is to feel ourselves as little naive children, basically sincere in our motives, but often stumbling over our feet or making mistakes because of our clumsiness. When we see children doing this, the parent in us easily forgives, even sees it as cute. Though we have larger bodies, we're still all children in the eyes of our Heavenly Father Mother. Not only is it a question of asking for forgiveness, we have to accept it as well. We're often like the child that cries and pouts even while our parents are loving and comforting us.

If we can enter the consciousness of the All-Wise and All-Loving Parent who sees all our actions as building blocks for our growth, whether abortion or anything else, we will be in the consciousness of forgiveness. It will blaze up within us as a fire that consumes all impurities, and it will pour down upon us as a waterfall that cleanses and heals.

thirteen

Parenting

Expansion of the Couple

A child is the base of the triangle of a family on which parents come together and love each other. In a family the wife and the husband are two individuals who are committed to each other forever. When they give birth to a child, however, the two sides of the triangle find a common base, strengthening the commitment in their marriage. The couple then feels responsible for their child as well as each other. The child is the product of both the father and the mother's physical, mental, emotional, and spiritual energies, so there is a natural bond between the child and the parents which can never be removed.

BABA HARI DASS

For almost every couple, the thought of bringing a child (or another child) into this world triggers a whole range of emotions. There can be a tremendous thrill of joy, and many couples are aware of this; but all too often this joy is covered by fear, doubt, or sadness.

Why so much heaviness around one of the richest experiences

life has to offer a couple?

Now with two children of our own, we are vividly aware of the several universal issues that almost sabotaged our own very deep desire to have children — issues that we have seen apply to many other couples. I mentioned fear, doubt, and sadness, but initially there really is only doubt, and doubt breeds fear and sadness.

What are the big doubts? And where do they come from? One of the deepest doubts arises out of all the pain and sorrow we've experienced in life, our remembrance of the "dark" side of our birth, infancy, childhood, puberty, adolescence, and so on. We've blocked out in various degrees the goodness, the love, the soul-growth. Yes, we do remember even our birth, although the memories may be mostly unconscious perhaps, and we've allowed the "negative" images of pain, or the jarring of our senses, to predominate over the far deeper and nobler feelings of, for example, triumph or mastery. This negative "take" on life, although really superficial, hangs us up and prevents us from seeing our deeper feelings, as well as the incredible opportunity for growth, mastery, and love that life offers. We too often get lost in the pain and sorrow, rather than seeing them in perspective, as stepping stones along the path to where we are now.

Personally, we were afraid of the tremendous responsibility of having a family. We had the illusion (as many do) that we would lose our freedom. We had visions of heavy chains binding us to the earth, weighing us down with worldliness. We didn't know then that our illusion of freedom was really irresponsibility and laziness. We didn't understand that the real freedom and happiness results from taking on responsibility gratefully.

Sometimes those of us on the path of consciousness make the mistake of twisting spiritual truth into rationalizations for not having children. We remember once deciding never to have children of our own because it was far better to feel that all children were our children. In reality we were tapping into deep spiritual truth, but rationalizing our fears nonetheless. Our other brilliant argument was: "We are all children, so why have children?" And it's true, our deepest desire is to become children, to become all that is childlike: open, trusting, simple, enthusiastic, forgiving, and loving. But, alas, we discovered these arguments all had doubt, fear, and selfishness hidden behind them. In her book, *Initiation,* Elizabeth Haich describes how during one of her initiations she got to a step that was impossibly high. She saw no way to mount it. It seemed hopeless. She then noticed someone else near her trying to scale the same steps. She forgot herself for a moment and helped the stranger up the steps. Imagine her surprise when she discovered she was at the top! The helping of another lifted her up without her even knowing it.

In our spiritual quest we can become very selfish, thinking only of our own growth or our relationship as a couple. We fail time after time to realize, as Saint Francis says, "It is in giving that we receive." We selfishly want liberation, or enlightenment, or love, but the only way to get these is to sacrifice our desires for them by helping the "strangers on the steps below us." We selfishly want to become children, but fail to realize that by giving love to our children, we are transformed most quickly. With God's help, we find ourselves less interested in our own "spiritual progress" and more interested in bringing the inner beauty and strength of our children to the surface, to help them become real servants of God. It is this that transforms us as well!

We put off having children a long time. Our first excuse was our education and professional training. Then there was a year and a half spiritual pilgrimage. Finally, there were no more excuses. We had to accept the fact that our desire to have children was blocked. We had always loved children very much and had vivid dreams about parenthood, but something was in the way. To one

wise being we tried to explain how beautiful our life was together, how we really didn't want it to change. He responded in perfect simplicity that nothing is constant, that our life will change anyway. That statement touched us very deeply.

Parenthood is a lot of work. Sometimes we get stuck just seeing the work of it all: the diapers, the disciplining, getting up in the middle of the night. It is then that we wonder why people glorify parenthood so much. But when we look deeper and feel all that we have been given in return, we know that it is one of life's most fulfilling endeavors. Our children have brought a closeness between the two of us that we never thought possible. The day after Rami was born we looked at each other as if for the first time. A whole new aspect of our beings had opened up for each of us to love — the father and mother.

We have seen so many individuals and couples place greater importance upon jobs, careers, and success than they do upon having children. The world (our worldly mind, that is) tells us that fame, sex, and power are more important. On a far more subtle level, our ego tells us our spiritual growth is more important than having children. There is much confusion and misunderstanding of the ancient teachings which say we must leave our family, husband, or wife. This was intended to mean we must leave our *attachment* to our family. Then, as well as now, we are being asked to changed our attitude about family life, not our physical involvement. In the same way, we are being asked to loosen our attachments to all of life, but only while we are participating *fully* in life. Many of us don't realize raising a family with love grounds us in a way that deepens our spiritual growth and our service to humanity.

Those of us who are open to the magic of pregnancy, birth, and family life, understand the powerful effect children have in the homes into which they come. Their deep love for us as parents is a force which magnifies our every thought and feeling, bringing everything to the surface to be processed in the light of awareness. We become sometimes painfully aware of our habits and negative tendencies. Our mistakes are revealed to us immediately, thus hastening the unfolding of our being. Joyce and I now see how Rami and Mira are forcing us to get our lives together. Many times it's not easy living with "consciousness barometers" who, with frustrating accuracy, reflect our every state of mind and feeling. Yet how very thankful we are to have such a wonderful opportunity for growth; to be exposed from our every hiding place. For when we enter the domain of the heart, with feelings of love, or gratitude, or blessing, usually that "little one" is right there with us, often as a very dear friend tenderly supporting us in our climb toward the light.

Ancient writings suggest that many children choose their

parents before incarnating. They speak of the intense preparation and assistance the child receives consciously in the higher realms, and the parents receive largely unconsciously (often in their sleep), for this well-planned reunion. Yes, reunion, for we need to be open to the possibility that we've all been together many times in many different roles. It's quite possible that Rami and Mira were shown before their births the perfection of the situation into which they would embark. They possibly knew all too well our every habit, the patterns of our blocked energy, the cause and effect of our every argument, and how these things would enhance their own growth. But then they would have also known our hearts, and would have seen the love and protection they would receive until they were on their own. In other words, it's a package deal. And we and all parents provide the optimal environment for what Rami and Mira and all children need — to learn, to grow, to master, and to love.

If the couple is committed, if they have consciously chosen to make their relationship a shared path to God, the arrival of a child will always expand their love. Their relationship will always be deepened, broadened. Rami and Mira have brought us ever new opportunities for expansion in our relationship. What we feared would be such a solemn sacrifice is becoming the thrill of giving. What we feared would become so burdensome a responsibility is proving to be our true freedom. What we feared would make us more worldly and materialistic is instead balancing us, steadying us, and planting our feet more firmly on the path of true spiritual unfoldment.

I remember once watching Joyce nurse Rami. How can I ever describe the experience — one of pure transformation affecting each one of us. I remember feeling bathed in the overflow of love. In this indescribably intimate energy-sharing between mother and child, I too was being nursed, and yes, was nursing as well. For the love welling up in my heart also protected and nourished my new family.

We feel that in pregnancy — almost more than at any other time in a woman's life — there is a need to be alone. A very high degree of sensitivity sets in as a woman advances in the stages of pregnancy. Women have reported that at times they can almost hear and feel the thoughts and feelings of those around them. In some parts of

Our Family

the world pregnant women are treated with great reverence as a result of this sensitivity and even the ability to perceive the future. It is in the times of solitude that you as a pregnant woman can tune into your own being and feel who you really are. We all need to love ourselves more, forgive ourselves more, and become our own best friend, so that when we are alone it is beautiful and fulfilling just to be with ourselves. What a wonderful gift to give your new child! For if you learn to love your own being, your child will naturally grow to love his or her own being. Once having contacted the place of fulfillment — your center — you can then give so much more to your mate, other children, friends, and the new baby. From this state of stillness and centeredness you can most easily contact the soul of the baby, and both send it love and receive its love in return. It is not necessary to spend long hours each day in retreat — though some pregnant women do and it is beautiful for them. It seems good to set aside one or two time-periods a day to practice the art of being alone — to practice stillness, receptivity, and centeredness. The ways we calm our minds and come into our hearts are individual and unique to us all.

What is important is that we do it. Taking time to be still and centered is the most rewarding, wonderful, and healthful practice you can do during pregnancy. For just the stilling of the activity of the body and mind will allow the higher impulses and Light to fill your consciousness. This will benefit the entire course of pregnancy and labor, physically and emotionally, and greatly benefit the baby as well as all those who have the privilege of being in your presence.

We would like to remind the man of the pregnant couple that you also are pregnant. The child is coming to you just as much as your wife. We feel that the two of you are chosen as a team, and are enfolded together in the aura of your child. A way that you can develop your fathering quality in your daily meditations is by surrounding your wife in light — providing a spiritual as well as physical protection for her and your child. Of course, this will greatly help you to open your heart and share in the joy of pregnancy.

The Initiation of Rami's Birth

It was 4 a.m. Thursday morning, March 25, 1976. Barry suddenly awoke and felt my huge belly. It was hard as a rock. He then heard a slight change in my breathing. Several minutes later the same thing happened. He leaned over, kissed me and said, ''You are in labor now.'' I thought he was kidding and laughed at him, thinking he was just overly excited. He told me his whole being was awake and alert to my labor and the nearness of the baby. I looked at him incredulously, and then stood up to go to the bathroom. Gush!! The waters broke all over the bedroom rug. Barry was right, I was in labor!

We lay in bed much too excited to sleep, not talking, just holding hands and feeling very close. I felt a strong Presence of the Mother God filling me with tremendous peace and love. I reflected on how the greatest lesson for me during the pregnancy had been in the area of forgiveness. When I was two months pregnant, in a moment of exhilaration I asked God to remove from me all negative feelings for others; that this baby might be nursed and cared for without my petty negativity toward other human beings. The asking had seemed so simple. The experiences that followed were not! I had allowed myself to become hurt by thoughtless, unkind words from two people concerning my pregnancy. I had found it impossible to forgive them.

This experience had been the source of much unhappiness in my pregnancy. Now I lay in bed and felt waves of compassion and love for them. As contractions came and went, the Presence of God continued to be strong. At that moment I realized that as I felt God's Presence more and more I would have less trouble forgiving others when they are unkind. People only act unkind out of a need to feel God themselves. I saw that these two people had no intention of hurting me. They were hurting themselves and needing love. In the Presence of God forgiveness is so easy. Negativity melts away and it becomes clear that we are all just little children wanting that same feeling of love. Contractions came and went. I squeezed Barry's hand and felt the resolution of and release from a long and difficult test.

Pregnancy offers an intensive opportunity for spiritual growth. Each pregnant woman experiences at least one test, i.e. lesson or initiation, to bring her closer to the consciousness of her baby. I felt so thankful for the lesson and test, thankful for the two people who had simply been used in the testing process. This had been a purification of lasting endurance...one of the many gifts from my child.

Barry rose at sunrise and stood naked in front of the open window as the first rays of sunlight hit his body. To me he was the most beautiful sight in the world. We both felt so very close to each other and so much in love. We had decided to do the labor and delivery entirely by ourselves, depending only on God's help. Most people discouraged us in this plan, saying that surely we would need extra hands to help. We had never wavered in our decision, however, knowing inwardly there was something we needed to learn, and it could only come from being alone.

We took a delightful walk in the woods and then returned to meditate, the contractions coming all the while. I remember those hours as such a blissful experience. Like most women laboring for the first time, I did everything I could to ease off the heavier contractions. I sat very still, moved cautiously and, as I later realized, slowed labor down, all the while holding a great pride that I was handling it all so well!

Twelve hours after the bag of waters broke, Barry finally looked at me and said, "Alright, we've had enough of this. It's time to work and have our baby. I'm going to give you an enema." I looked at him communicating both my pain and trust. I happen to be one of those people that hate enemas. It turned out to be quite a difficult experience, but it did bring me right into heavy labor. Contractions came strong and heavy, and I needed Barry's total attention in order to cope. After a time, I got comfortable with the degree of intensity. Then he looked at me with the kind of love that pushes the beloved into harder things and said to me, "Now we are going for a walk in the woods." My eyes pleaded and yet his eyes were steady and confident, so off we went for a three-quarter-mile walk. The contractions would come so strongly that I leaned my body on Barry's, he became my strength, and we became as one.

When we returned from the walk it was dark and cold. Barry started a fire in our living room fireplace, and I sat in front of it working alone with the contractions while he prepared things for the delivery. It was hard to be alone and in heavy labor. I needed to call on every inner strength I possessed. Barry returned and we settled into a nice rhythm. The contractions came with immense force. He sat behind me applying pressure to my back, and for the resting phase he held me and gave me much love and support.

Around 9 p.m. it seemed to us both that I had entered the tran-

sition period. Barry made this entry in my journal afterwards:
"I started to feel very high, that wonderful feeling of God-
Presence. I was filled with assurance that all events were being
guided. I definitely knew for the first time that everything would
go well. The last remnants of doubt burned away in that moment.
Joyce picked up on my feelings and we felt very close — and felt our
gratitude to God."

I had read that transition is usually the hardest and shortest
part of labor, so I gave it my all. Wave after wave of contractions
came and we worked as a team. I felt united with Barry. We were
truly experiencing all this as one being. A normal transition is
usually well under an hour. After two hours had gone by, we
wondered if something was wrong. Barry examined me and said it
felt like a lip of the cervix was holding up the progress. He tried
massaging it which seemed to help a little. We went back to our
spot by the fire and worked more as a team. The contractions,
however, diminished in intensity. Barry tried a second exam and
massage, but nothing happened. The uterus slowed down even
further.

At this point I looked deeply into his eyes. That complete
strength and self-confidence was gone. He was very pale and said
to me, "Come, we have to go to the hospital." Being a nurse who
has seen many drug-induced hospital births, my fear was the opposite to that of most women. There was no way I was going to the
hospital. Until that point, Barry had been the one with the strength
taking care of me. From then on, that strength would alternate between us, each of us in turn feeling weak while the other was
strong.

I gently said to him, "Barry, we can do it. Let's pray and ask
for help, and surrender this birth to God." We prayed and that
seemed to help us both, though the contractions were still very
slight. We both felt like innocent and helpless children, waiting for
our Divine Mommy to come and take care of us. Gone was the
pride in doing this birth by ourselves. We knew we were totally
dependent upon a higher source. This feeling was to continue
throughout the rest of the labor.

We tried walking again, but the labor didn't pick up. It was as
if the baby were waiting for something before she would begin to
descend the birth channel. Barry suddenly looked at me with profound love and said, "What is it" You know inside what is stopping labor." His face was pale and worn, yet in that moment his
voice was used by a Greater Voice. As he spoke, something broke

within me and I burst into tears. A flow of unconscious fears surfaced. Barry and I had spoken of these fears intellectually, but they had never been cleared in my feelings. Through my tears I blurted out, "I don't know if I really want this baby. What if it changes the love and closeness between us? Other fathers have said they were always jealous of the children. Maybe you will be too. Oh, Barry I love you so much. I can't bear thinking that another will come and perhaps our closeness will go."

During my pregnancy I had always been very excited and enthusiastic about having a baby. These fears would come up every once in awhile, but I would push them aside as silly. Here they were in full view, and our baby wasn't about to come until I dealt with them on the spot.

It was at this point that one of the peak experiences of our life took place. There was my beloved husband, weary from helping me through twenty hours of labor. I knew that he did not have it in him at that point to speak with such wisdom. Yet when he spoke, it was the voice of a master speaking through him, and divine wisdom poured out. We heard through Barry's lips of the great blessing it is to be chosen as "care-takers" of a New Age child, i.e. a being coming to help bring in an age of enduring peace, coming with a very high consciousness and love. Just being in the presence of such a one, the voice told us, will speed our own spiritual journey tremendously. We were told that the child's coming would increase the closeness between the two of us, and her presence in our lives would bring us closer to God. There would be no jealousy, since our selfishness would be replaced by true giving, and in giving we would receive more than we could ever dream.

When the words stopped we both felt happy and inspired. The air had been cleared! Ever so gently, by herself, Rami started her descent down the birth channel. We knew she had heard and was satisfied that we understood.

The pushing stage of labor was quite an ordeal because the cervix had apparently become sore. We worked together for three more hours. During that time we alternately felt a period of weakness and wanting to give up, while the other was able to be strong and help.

Finally her head emerged and Barry reported, "He is born." (We were *so* certain of having a boy.) He told me later that Rami came out with her eyes fully opened and instantly locked gaze with him. He described it this way: "The moment her head was born was one of those magical moments that can never be adequately described in words. I gently turned her head and found myself looking directly into the eyes of an old and very wise being, as well as a newborn baby. But the feeling that stood out the most strongly was one of mutual recognition...not only me recognizing her, but she also acknowledging our friendship. I was awed by her awakeness.''

One more push and the baby was out, twenty-five hours after the waters broke. Barry then informed me, ''We have a little girl.'' I will never forget the thrill of divine joy that passed through my body. I had wanted a girl so much I hadn't even dared hope for one. Then he gently placed her upon me and we both experienced the greatest joy we have ever known. Her look was so intent, so steady, so filled with love for us both. She never cried! The only sound in the room was a faraway sweet sound of angels singing. That moment more than made up for any pain experienced. Now we were a family. Welcome beloved baby! We love you so much!

I had never felt so much love in my entire life. I looked at Barry and he was no longer a being outside of me. He was within me, and the love we felt for each other touched the depths of the universe.

Ah such bliss! But what goes up must come down, and our bliss was short-lived. I had one of those rare complications in which the placenta doesn't come out, and I had a steady flow of blood. My mother had experienced the same difficulty delivering me. Reluctantly we put our precious bundle down and worked several more hours, squatting, pulling, and praying. Barry was at the point of exhaustion and the fear he once again felt made his thinking process cloudy. We both knew I was slipping into shock because of loss of blood. Within me, I felt I could easily drift off and leave my body. The presence of angels was so strong it would have been easy to leave my body and join the spirit world. Just as I felt myself beginning to slip, a strong and steady voice resounded within me. "*Stop!* Either go to the hospital or seek help immediately!"

That same voice that commanded me to alertness then commanded Barry into action, and once again we felt God's command over the situation. We called a doctor experienced in home birth. He was a deeply spiritual man and a friend of Barry's. He came right over and told us he had been praying the entire time as this situation can be quite dangerous. We prayed together, and then, with a technique only hundreds of home births can provide, out came the placenta. As a tender good shepherd would do, he took care of everything for us and sweetly bid us all sleep for awhile. Before he left he said a prayer of blessing for Rami. The three of us lay in bed and slept all day — sweet, sweet sleep.

When I awoke, Barry and Rami were still sleeping. How heavenly to see them both. I got up, went outside, and lay down on a blanket to watch the sun setting. I couldn't help feeling a little sad inside. Somehow I was equating the difficulty of the labor with failure of some kind. My labor with Rami was more difficult than most women experience. I asked God why it had been so hard for me. Perhaps because I was so vulnerable and open, the reply came immediately and strongly:

"God provides the greatest opportunities for growth to those who deeply ask."

I saw and felt how I was needing everything I received to make me stronger, to bring Barry and me to a point of complete dependence upon God, and to bring us closer in a way that could not have been achieved in any other way. The sadness was replaced by extreme gratefulness, and to this day I feel thankful for every precious minute of that labor experience.

The Call to Service

Behold the Handmaiden of the Lord.

MOTHER MARY

The gift of motherhood is truly divine. Various spiritual teachers and masters have written that there is no greater service than to raise and guide a child's footstep toward God. What greater gift can we possibly give the world, than to give it a child who is balanced physically and emotionally and has learned attunement to the Light, thus helping to raise the vibrations of the entire planet? The responsibility and joy in this type of sevice is awesome. However, for many women the task of accepting this service is at times rather difficult.

As I sit to write, I gaze down upon my growing abdomen and see waves of movement as my baby dances within me. I am seven months pregnant. How I love this little one. From the other room I hear Rami, now 5½ years old, playing. She is pretending to be an angel and has dressed herself up in her pink nightgown and cardboard wings. She "flies" about her room singing to her dolls that God loves them. Her sweet voice fills our home with joy. I feel another kick from the blessed one inside and truly my heart feels as if it will overflow with love and gratitude to be a mother. But as I sit and relish this moment of fulfillment, memories and pictures of hard times come flowing to me. These were times when I resented and resisted the changes motherhood brings, and brought suffering upon myself. There will probably be more hard times ahead as I learn to give up selfishness and truly give.

Some women seem to flow quite naturally into motherhood. There is no struggle. They seem to accept all the changes beautifully. For myself, and I believe for most women, there is some degree of struggle.

When I entered college in 1964, I knew I would dedicate my life to children. I had always felt a deep attunement to them. My nursing and graduate education strongly emphasized this. I was still simple and just wanted to help children be themselves. However, as I gained experience, my jobs became more and more prestigious. I began to enjoy a feeling of importance which subtly started taking over my simple ideals of helping children. At one point I was in charge of a program for emotionally disturbed children and had great responsibility with 30 staff members under my direction. My ego was feeling quite important and, before I knew it, my career was of paramount interest. I began looking ahead to greater and greater advancement in position, rather than greater opportunities of serving children.

Fortunately for me, a hidden blessing came in the form of an unexpected move to Oregon, where Barry could go on to psychiatric residency training. There, Barry worked fifty to eighty hours a week at the hospital. Alone in a small house in the Oregon woods, I gradually grew to see just how far away I had strayed from my original goal. Self-importance had taken priority over true service.

When we left Oregon, Barry and I began a spiritual journey which lasted two years. We traveled all over and studied with various spiritual teachers. We then moved to Santa Cruz where we began our joint practice in counseling and became pregnant with our first child. I loved every minute of the counseling work, and at times even forgot that a baby might bring changes in my life. Whenever I would think about the possible changes I'd get a little panicky, and then just decide I'd hire babysitters right away. Self-importance had crept in again and I was failing to see the service that God was intending for me to do.

The joy and bliss of Rami's coming faded slowly after about one month, and I was faced with the day-to-day care. I worked full time right up until six hours before labor started, and I tried to go back to work 14 days later. However, it became increasingly clear that I had to give up the work. I tried taking Rami with me while I counseled people, but it didn't work. Her sensitivity toward others and her environment was extreme. If someone expressed the slightest negativity, Rami would cry. If we took her some place and the vibrations weren't peaceful, she would scream in agony until we brought her home. Barry tried watching her while I saw people in counseling. However, if I did not properly clear my aura from the person's energy, Rami would sense it immediately, scream, and be unable to nurse. It became apparent that I had to give up my work altogether for a while and devote myself totally to surrounding Rami with a peaceful, loving environment.

At first my ego screamed and cried for deliverance. There was no feeling of importance or recognition from others — just the simple day-to-day tasks of caring for an infant. In my heart I knew I was doing what God wanted of me. Yet the voice of my heart was still soft in comparison to the screams of my mind. Week after week, month after month, however, my heart grew stronger, and

the demands of my mind lessened. Caring for Rami was teaching me the way of love. I was learning to truly give. I was just beginning to understand what it means to be a servant of God, asking only to do His will.

One morning when Rami was six months old, I awakened with a sense of perfect fulfillment and joy. The day that stretched before me was the same as any other: love and care of Rami. Barry was scheduled to see six persons, all of whom were my favorites when we were counseling together. As I gazed at the schedule I waited for that usual pang of jealousy I had felt upon seeing Barry go off to do what I thought was "more important" work. Instead, that feeling had been replaced by gratitude to be able to be with Rami.

As I was nursing her later in the day, my heart felt overwhelmed with love. Suddenly a Presence and soft light filled the room. I felt inside that this is what God is wanting me to do right now with my life. A voice seemed to speak inside me saying, "There is no greater service you can be doing right now than loving and caring for your child." Then, in affirmation of what had been said within, I heard a faint but distinct sound of angels singing. I had only heard this sound once before, when Rami was born. No amount of career importance or worldly recognition could have equalled that moment. I knew the fulfillment and joy that comes from doing God's will.

You may be used at any moment for the Master's service, but because the call to service is not always what you were expecting, sometimes you do not realize that you have been called and chosen for the Masters' work. Make ready in your hearts, for you know not the day nor the hour when the Master will come.

WHITE EAGLE

fourteen

The Gift of Receiving

Humble yourself to receive before you can truly give

AMERICAN INDIAN SAYING

I was eight and a half months pregnant with our second daughter, feeling very bulky, and very much wanting to be alone. Several months previously, however, I had signed up for a workshop to complete my nursing credits before our baby came. Now I didn't want to go. In fact, the thought of going was so distasteful to me that I found myself getting sick — my body's feeble attempt at an excuse. I was all set to call and cancel when I decided to still myself and ask for inner guidance. "Go," said the gentle voice within, "there is something you are needing to learn before the baby comes."

That evening I dragged my large form to the university to begin the 2½ day workshop. What was I needing to learn? I felt so ready for the baby to come, and didn't really feel I needed anything more. As I was driving up the hill to the school, I realized

148

partly why I felt reluctant. I felt I couldn't give very much. My energy had turned almost entirely inward. I was more conscious of how our baby was doing than I was of others. What would it be like to be with a group of people in this way, and not be giving to them?

There were forty participants: doctors, nurses, and paraprofessionals, all meeting to learn more about healing. I spent most of the first day of the workshop wondering why God had sent me there, and wishing I were home lying in the sun. Finally, the leader started talking about receiving, and a little knock came from my heart. I heard within, "This is for you, this is why I sent you." The leader pointed out that those of us in the helping professions tend to be givers. Few of us know how to truly receive. Later I realized the significance of his message. Until we deeply learn to receive from our mates, children, those we serve, and from all beings we contact, we cannot truly give.

Learning to receive is a three-step process. First, as small children we want only to receive, the "give me, what did you bring me, I want, he has more than I do" consciousness. Then, if we are fortunate enough to have loving parents and guiding hands, we learn it is more blessed to give than to receive. Finally, when that concept is fully established, we must come back to receiving and balance the two.

Receiving is a delicate art that must be practiced in all relationships. There must be the proper balance between giving to each other and receiving from each other. This balance can then bring forth a beautiful wheel of growth and harmony.

Receiving is very different from the ego-consciousness of "getting," the awareness of getting enough to fulfill our expectations each moment. "Getting" depends upon the other person doing, saying, or giving something. Receiving is the conscious activity of opening the heart to draw in the divine from another, ie. that which is pure and good. By allowing ourselves to enter into a state of receptivity, we can be open to hearing feeling, and sensing the Presence of God coming through another. This is one of the highest gifts we can give one another. Whether or not the person is aware of how you are perceiving them at that moment, unconsciously it will be felt, and will serve to uplift them. By practicing this art with those we contact, we likewise will learn to receive from the many other beings who are guiding and strengthening us.

The workshop turned out to be a very positive experience for me. Rather than concentrating on what I could give each person, or what I could teach them, or how I could outwardly serve them, I concentrated on what I could receive and how I could learn from each individual. I listened intently as each person spoke to me in the various discussion periods. I learned from each person, and enjoyed seeing how God was manifesting through them. In my openness to each, I had also given.

Several days later a man came to see me for counseling. I had seen him several times a year for about four years. He was also a counselor, who was having difficulty with his wife, and therefore sought a female opinion. Though I loved this man very much, I didn't look forward to seeing him. The sessions were always very hard for me since there seemed to be an ever-present power struggle over who was going to counsel who. We began the session with a little meditation. As we sat together, I felt the impulse to just sit and receive, rather than try to get my point across, teach him, or even counsel him. I asked him to tell me what was happening in his life, then I just sat back and drank in his beauty, strength, and love. He sensed the change and began to open up to me as never before. The more receptive I became to him, the more deeply he opened up, until he was in tears and all that he was needing to see came to him by his own opening process. I felt exhilarated and in awe of what had happened. It had been a break-through not only for him, but for me as well.

There is great power in receiving. Many of us feel we are only performing good deeds when we are outwardly serving, doing, or giving. Sometimes the highest act can be to open and receive from another. Those who come to us for help have as much to give to us as we have to give to them. Likewise, we have as much to receive and learn from our mate as we have to give. There is always a balance.

In 1972, Barry and I were indeed having a difficult time in our marriage. He was very involved with finishing medical school. I had an important job and the power was going to my head. I felt not only important, but indispensable as well. We had a major conflict in our relationship and I was thinking seriously of leaving Barry. I thought that my job was giving me more than my marriage. My body gave me all kinds of signals that I was on the wrong track, but I ignored them. Finally one night I sensed I was going the wrong way — I hadn't really prayed in several years, but that night I asked God to show me my mistakes.

My answer came the next day in an interesting form. I hadn't wanted to be with Barry for the weekend so I went off with a friend to the beach. My dog was attacked by another dog and, in attempting to help him, my finger was bitten. The next day my hand was a useless claw. The infection was spreading down the bone of my finger, threatening to cause the loss of my entire hand. Later I lay in a hospital bed, totally helpless. The infected hand was suspended above me for drainage, while the other was immobilized by the various I.V. tubes. I could do nothing but lay there. Barry came each day, fed me, and cared for me. I was being forced to receive from him.

As the days wore on, my heart opened more and more to him. The job, the feeling of power, were nothing in comparison to his love. I realized how little time I had allowed myself to simply receive from him. Moreover, I had allowed little time to receive of God's love and protection. So busy out in the world, giving, helping, doing, being the big shot, I had not taken time to feel God's precious gifts.

As Barry sat with me each day, he also realized how little he had been receiving from me, and how great the need was for this in our relationship. We began practicing and exploring realms of receptivity to each other. This was the turning point in our marriage, and the conscious beginning of our spiritual path.

I remember seeing a woman a while ago — the super-woman type. She drove a big produce truck and could unload a truck full of orange crates faster than any man. She was an excellent plumber, mechanic, carpenter, weaver, mother and leader of a spiritual group. It seemed the only thing she could not do well was stay in a relationship. There was a man she loved very much, and wanted desperately to make a relationship work. However, the usual destructive patterns were beginning, and the man was drifting away.

Suddenly, her father became very ill and had only a few days to live. This woman loved her father very much and immediately traveled with her boyfriend to be with him. The night that he was dying, she and her boyfriend sat very close to him. Her grief and emotions threatened to overwhelm her. She turned to her boyfriend in a fully receptive state and said, "Help me." He rose to her need with great strength. She had never seen him be so beautiful before. He later told her that, though it was indeed a sad time, he had never felt closer to her. It was the first time in their relationship that she asked for help, and had been fully receptive to him. In that moment she had given him the highest gift of love.

   As we practice receiving from one another, we realize we are all teaching each other, as well as needing each other. God's guidance can come from the greatest spiritual teacher or from the smallest child. It is up to us to be receptive. Sometimes this can happen through the major events of our life, or sometimes through an everyday occurrence. In the rush and busy-ness of the day's schedule, take a moment to stop and see the beauty of each member of your family, or those you are with at the moment. As you feel their beauty you will receive so much, plus you will help raise the consciousness of all.

   Throughout the remaining two weeks of my pregnancy, I steadily practiced receiving. It seemed our baby was wanting to teach me a deep lesson, and prepare me for an ultimate test.

   September 21, 1981 *(Journal entry written ten hours before I unexpectantly went into labor with Mira Naomi)*

   "As I sit alone I reflect on the pregnancy and all it has meant to me. I feel at one with all pregnant women, and feel the specialness of this sacred time in our lives. Pregnancy is both joy and pain, sweetness and sorrow. If you invite a spiritual being into your life, then there is no such thing as a smooth, completely joyful pregnancy. This being is coming from a higher plane of consciousness, and we as women must be strengthened and raised to meet our child. The strengthening and purifying process is

sometimes difficult; the rewards are always great, always wor-
thwhile. I often feel that there is no faster way to grow spiritually
than to invite one of these beacons of light into your life.''

The waters broke in the middle of the night and labor began.
The baby was so peaceful, coming down with such gentleness and
love. Several dear women friends arrived in the morning and
helped prepare our home for labor. Flower petals were spread
everywhere, dried lavender blossoms burned with sweet aroma,
and delicate herbs hung here and there. I felt like a queen
commanding a great show. I told the women and Barry what to do
and they scurried here and there. Then I led us all in a meditation,
and Barry read something I felt inspired to write the day before:

> The contractions come and go now. Sweet baby, you are pushing
> down upon me so gently and asking me to surrender to love and
> open the door. I feel your head opening my body. I feel your spirit
> opening my soul to more light. How can I ever thank you for all
> you have taught me in these nine months. You showed me where
> I am selfish, and quietly asked me to give that up. You helped me
> experience not only my Mother-God, but also my Father-God.
> Then you insisted with all the strength of your being that I call
> upon them more and dwell more in their Presence. You scolded
> me gently (and not so gently) when I strayed. My body went
> through all kinds of physical pains and joys as you grew within
> me, and you reminded me constantly to see it all as purification,
> and to be grateful. You helped me feel my beauty, and experience
> God in such a deep, inner way. And now you push upon me and
> ask me to open and set you free. I feel your joy and excitement to
> begin your work upon the earth. I thank you for all you have
> given me in these nine months that we have lived as one. As I sur-
> render to the love that you are, I pray that you continue to teach
> me and help me to grow.

I was 5 centimeters dilated, feeling wonderful and still in command of the whole show. I got up to get a drink of water and felt
like dancing the entire way. Then a very strong contraction jumped
me to 7 centimeters. That was to signal my last break for two and a
half hours. I somehow made it to the birthing area as strong contractions followed one after another. There was only a one or two
second break until the next contraction came pounding upon me
again. The commanding queen was now like a small child, totally
dependent upon others' direction and support.

As I neared transition, my thinking process went blank. There was no time to sit back and feel and digest the experience. The entire life force within me was absorbed by the continual stream of strong contractions. Without being able to think, or to feel inwardly, my ultimate test in receptivity came. Before the peak of a tidal-wave-like contraction, I somehow managed to cry out to Barry, "Be my thinking...be my feeling...be my inner voice." And so for two hours he became my psychological and spiritual self, talking outloud to me gently, reminding me of all I needed. His voice became my own still, small voice that I had grown so dependent upon throughout the years while, at the same time, he took charge of the labor and delivery. The women intuitively responded to all my physical needs. I could do nothing but flow with the constant wave of contractions, and receive fully the love and protection of God coming through their hands and voices. Then came the final two pushes and our precious daughter was with us.

The experience of such complete dependence and receptivity has completely changed my life. As I looked at my dear sweet baby, into the eyes of Barry, and then at the dear women, I knew in that moment we are all one being. Our lives and spiritual growth are dependent upon our receptivity to others. To grow toward oneness, we must reach out to the Divine in others and receive it into our being.

Sweet Mira Naomi, you are only five minutes old, and already you have taught me a deep and lasting lesson.

fifteen

Our Home Within

Lay not up for yourselves treasures upon earth...for where your treasure is, there will your heart be also.

JESUS

What you are looking for is who is looking.

SAINT FRANCIS

The nesting impulse is deeply ingrained in couples. In addition to this, shelter is one of humanity's basic needs for survival. This simple impulse and need often get blown up out of proportion and the physical home becomes of paramount importance. Sometimes the desire for a beautiful home becomes the chief goal in life, replacing the greater need for love, harmony and peace.

Some time ago, Barry and I decided we might like to buy our own home. I remember one lovely home we visited on a large piece of property with a view of the ocean. Outwardly everything seem ed just perfect, yet as we walked to the front door we were both struck by a growing feeling of sadness. A pleasant man, the owner and builder, opened the door and showed us around the house. Though much care was put into every detail of the construction, the house lacked warmth. Noticing several of the bedrooms were for children, we inquired about them. The man suddenly started crying and explained that his wife had left with the children and was filing for a divorce. They had put all their energy into building the perfect house and had neglected nourishing each other. Their dream house was built, but their relationship was demolished.

We encountered similar situations in over half of the homes we looked at. In some cases it was the wife who had gotten lost in the outward beauty and manifestation, and the husband left. In other instances it was the male taking pride in building that caused the wife to leave out of loneliness. It was as if either or both were having an affair with a cement, wood and glass partner.

The homes that endure are built upon love, harmony, truth, respect, gentleness, and peace. With these building materials the simplest structure can become a golden temple where all who enter are blessed.

There is a lovely story about a wealthy man who lived in a magnificent dwelling on earth. He devoted his full time to making his home more and more beautiful. He concentrated so much upon this task, however, that he seldom thought of, or helped, another person. Finally his life ended and the angel of death came to take him to his heavenly home. They passed many beautiful and wealthy homes with lovely gardens. "Surely this is where I will live now," thought the man. But the angel took him further along past poorer and poorer homes. Finally they came to the end of the line and the angel pointed to a primitive shack which was barely held together. The man complained, "I am a wealthy man. I cannot live there." "I'm sorry sir," the angel replied, "we did the best we could with the materials you sent us."

The feeling of love and harmony is of far greater importance than the physical structure in which we live. This feeling transforms any place or situation into a temple of light. Some years ago Barry and I had a profound experience that reinforced this lesson. Barry will describe it:

In July of 1973 I "dropped out" of my professional training after one year of psychiatry at the University of Oregon Medical Center in Portland. We rented a cabin on the densely-forested western slope of Mt. Hood, where we felt we could intensify our spiritual practices accompanied by the nearby roar of the glacial-fed Zigzag River. It was a magnificent spot — until autumn came, the sun dipped down below the tree tops, and it grew cold and increasingly wet. By the end of November, after thirty solid days of rain (a record even for Oregon), and our worsening depression, we realized it was time to leave. But where? Where was home? Not in New York or Buffalo with our parents and relatives. Oregon? Beautiful, but just not home.

Somehow we decided to travel south into Mexico for the winter. We ended up on a very remote beach one mile from a tiny Mexican Village named, of all places, San Francisco. We spent six weeks reading and studying our spiritual books, trying to meditate, sometimes succeeding. We swam and walked and lived on simple foods. But, alas, this too was not home, although we learned a great many things, and had many profound experiences.

We headed North once again. We spent a week visiting relatives and friends in Los Angeles, where we were hit many times with the inevitable, "Where are you going to live?" and "What are you going to do?". Thoroughly confused, we again sought the mountains. By the time we reached the Kern River Highway, I was depressed and Joyce was in tears. We were approaching a picnic area, so I pulled in and turned off the motor. I held Joyce and tried to comfort her as she sobbed the words, "I feel so far away from home. I want a home." We sat there a long time in the lengthening afternoon shadows, Joyce either crying or asking God and me for help. I felt helpless in my attempts to reassure her that it would all work out somehow. Deep down I knew it would, but my own doubts held me captive. Yet at least I could hold her.

Finally, I insisted we take a walk. We left the car and proceeded down the hill to the river. Joyce found a rock to sit on, where she could be alone to quiet her feelings. I wandered upstream a few hundred feet. Walking in the woods has always helped me. I remembered where we lived when I was a psychiatry resident, the rural Tualatin Hills of Northwest Portland. At the end of the numerous frustrating days on the psychiatry ward, where I wasn't allowed to do what my heart told me was right for my patients, I could drive a half hour home and walk amid my beloved Douglas fir trees. There somehow I could trade my tensions with the peacefulness of the trees. They never seemed to mind.

Here too, along the Kern River, I was beginning to feel more serene. I must have been looking at the ground, for I didn't notice it until I was within a few feet. There, directly in front of me, carved on a tree in big bold letters enclosed in a heart, were the words: *"JOYCE, HOME IS JUST A FEELING."*

At first I couldn't believe my eyes. I looked around in amazement. No one around! Then it struck me this was real and actually happening to me. It would have been much easier for me had the carver omitted the name. But no, the impact had to be direct and hard...and very personal!

My legs felt strangely wobbly, and I really don't know if I was laughing or crying as I ran to get Joyce. Without a word, and to her surprise, I led her back to the tree. Yes! It was still there. Joyce was transfixed, and in silence together we thanked God for this miracle.

My mind still has trouble with this experience. I've hardly ever seen carvings on a tree much different than "John loves Mary" or "Frank was here." This message was so intimately personal. I had my camera in the car, but it seemed so very out of place to record all this on film. Our hearts had been permanently imprinted. It didn't matter whether the carving was done with human hands or was materialized just for us. What mattered was that God led us to this tree, and is leading us still. Since that moment, we have been in the process of looking within for the feeling of home. Where we live outwardly is becoming less and less important. We still have a long way to go, but how wonderful to remember that signpost, that our true home, the Kingdom of Heaven, is a feeling within.

The Kingdom of Heaven is within you...

Seek ye first the Kingdom of Heaven,
and all things will be added unto you.

JESUS

sixteen

Christmas and Easter Initiations

The Christmas Initiation

Christmas is a time for giving. We can give materially, but we can also give spiritually. The spiritual gifts which come from the heart have the greatest effect on the receiver as well as the giver. A deeply-felt spiritual gift can make a relationship blossom into the flower it was intended to be.

A young woman once came for counseling a week before Christmas. She was obviously uptight about something, yet she had no idea what it was. We talked about the usual things that tended to upset her, but we drew a blank. Finally, we asked how her Christmas plans were going, and she burst into tears. Through deep sobs she related how she, her husband, and child were planning to attend a big family reunion in Los Angeles. People were coming from all over, trying to make this the best Christmas reunion of all. Loving her family very much, she wanted to help make it very special but had no money left to buy anyone a present. Nor did she have any time to make special presents as her toddler kept her very busy. She cried and cried, feeling for certain she would offend people by her lack of giving.

We then talked about spiritual gifts and how these can be the most beautiful of all. She went home and wrote a simple poem. In it she described what she appreciated the most about each member of her family, and the way that quality had helped her grow. Before the Christmas dinner she read the poem to everyone. Needless to say, all were in tears. Her poem had been the most special part of Christmas.

The gift of appreciation is a powerful one. Our mates need this so much more than a new sweater or slippers. Our hearts need one person to see past all of our games and habits, to see the being we are meant to be. We all need someone to stand by us and see our beauty. We flower when God sees our beauty through human eyes.

Christmas is also a time of reunion. People go to great effort and expense to be reunited with others. One year we felt particularly sad, because both of our families would be having gatherings on the east coast. We would be alone with our first baby daughter. There was no one to reunite with. We felt quite lonely. Then the day before Christmas we realized we could reunite with each other. We could concentrate on a reunion of our souls by focusing on the purity, innocence, and beauty in one another. On Christmas Eve we sat opposite each other and lit candles. We took turns revealing all the things about the other that we appreciated the most. With each shared statement of beauty about the other, a new door was opened and we could see a little more clearly into the perfection of our Christ-Selves. That was a reunion I shall never forget, the power of which lingered all year.

An expression of appreciation seems so simple, so humble, yet if deeply felt, can be the most powerful gift. Through the warmth and glow of human love for one another, the heart is opened even wider to allow the light of the Cosmic Christ to enter and dwell therein. Thus the true Christmas spirit is observed by the simplest and humblest of gifts.

The Winter Solstice, and especially Christmas, parallels a most important initiation in all deep relationships. At this time of year the sun is at its lowest point; the planet earth in its darkest period. It corresponds to those times of greatest darkness with our loved ones, when we reach a point of true despair, the point of giving up perhaps. This doesn't necessarily correspond with the seasons. It may happen at any time. It may be happening to you now! It is a time of dying. The old ways of relating must eventually become stagnant and then die. It is a time of pain — not because dying is painful, but because we resist dying, clinging to worn-out roles and games, clinging to comfort and security. The pain comes from the resistance.

Yet die we must, if we are to keep growing, indeed, keep living. Ask the tree if it tries to hold on to its dead leaves in the autumn, or if it feels pain in letting them go. Nicholas Herman, as a young soldier in seventeenth century France, saw a leafless tree in the winter and realized how it would burst with new life in the spring. He at once became filled with such love and spiritual longing that he entered the barefoot Carmelite Order and became the God-intoxicated Brother Lawrence. He was shown what the sufis refer to as "dying before you die," or birth already contained within death.

At the time of the winter solstice, at the time of greatest darkness and death, comes Christmas, the birth of the Christ, which is the birth of the Light in our hearts. This is always how it is. The Master Jesus was born at a time of very great darkness in our planet's history, as well as at the winter solstice. Many other prophets and avatars came in similar conditions. There is something very universal about this. The night is always darkest just before the dawn.

In our relationships with our husbands and wives, our dearest friends, our parents or children, we must all go through these dark nights. We must all experience the frustration, hopelessness and despair of ever finding love through our own intellects and personalities, of getting it our own way and by ourselves. It is only then that we cry out for help and become humbled. Then, like the lowly stable and cave where Jesus was born, the Christ-Light can be born in our humbled heart-caves. It comes from knowing we can only depend on God, whether it's regarding a relationship or anything else in life. This great love comes from admitting our helplessness and asking for help. Love can be born in our hearts only if we sincerely ask for help. This help only comes from God, the Great Spirit, yet God is often most accessible through our loved ones. This is one of the greatest secrets of transforming relationships: those closest to us can often be the greatest channels of Divine Love. This requires the wisdom of being open, the spirit of receptivity, and is one of the highest gifts we can give each other.

May the Christ be born in you now!

The Easter Initiation

The meaningfulness of crucifixion and the hope of resurrection are universal phenomena. Those who follow any spiritual path can relate to the inner significance of this time and be inspired. Easter is a time of renewal, a time of once again seeing our purpose here on Earth. We are not here to become buried under the cross of matter or, in the case of our relationships, to become weighed down by the heaviness of our own limitations. We are here to experience being fully immersed in the world, yet learn to fly together into realms of light and love. The essence of Easter gives us hope that we can rise even higher and experience ever more joy together.

The following Easter initiation ceremony can be done any day of the year:

Bring a sheet of paper, a pencil, matches, a place to burn the paper, and a candle. Sit facing each other. Close your eyes and practice taking deep breaths together. With each out-breath, feel as if you are letting go of tensions, negative thoughts and areas where you are blocked in loving. With each in-breath experience your body being filled with light. When you feel an attunement with each other, open your eyes and feel your love.

Now search your heart for an area of your relationship that needs to die. This could be a limitation you've imposed upon yourself or your relationship, a grudge you are holding, a way you hold back love, a jealousy, etc. Perhaps you will each choose a separate problem, or choose one together. When there is an agreement on that aspect of your relating that needs to go, write it down on the paper.

Now hold the paper together and close your eyes. Let one of you or both of you say a prayer out loud asking for help and strength to let this aspect of your relationship go. Next, crumple the paper together. As you do this, feel love for this part that is needing to die. Areas of our personality which block the flow of love do not leave by hating them away. They fade through love, patience, and tolerance for ourselves and for one another.

Now open your eyes and light the paper with a match. As it burns, take your candle and together take light from the burning paper. The fire of crucifixion kindles the Light of resurrection. Therefore, feel the aspect of your relating that is being resurrected with you, the positive quality that is being transformed from the negative.

As we ask with sincerity, so do we receive. We must always keep in our hearts the promise of the resurrection: with God's help we can rise above limitations and be transformed.

I am your Friend who, though invisible to you, walks with you and helps you. Feel that you can call on Me. I will not perform a miracle for you, but I AM the Light within you which is the miracle performing all things.

SAINT GERMAIN

seventeen

Death in the Relationship

I shall have this good at least, that till death I shall have done all that is in me to love God.

BROTHER LAWRENCE

I am the ocean
I am the waves
The boat goes through
I am dying with you

SONG WRITTEN BY RAMI, AGE 4

The death of a lifetime partner may occur at any time. When it does, it is always a major test of your love...and faith. Especially for the one "left behind", the grief, sorrow, indeed, the whole process, provides an opportunity for tremendous spiritual growth.

Some years ago, a young woman with four children made an appointment to see me. The story she told went back a few mo-

years to a time when she lived with her husband and children on a small island off the coast of Ireland. There were definite strains upon their relationship, a major one being another woman living with them, but the love of this couple was genuine.

In order to get supplies and food it was necessary for them to cross the channel to the mainland in a small boat. On one such day the wind seemed stronger than usual. The woman tried to discourage her husband from making the trip, but he was still determined, and set off with a friend. By late afternoon the boat was heavily loaded and the water was peaked with whitecaps. The two men stood on the mainland shore, contemplating the return trip home.

The day had been more frustrating than usual for the woman, and fatigue opened the door to negative thoughts. When it started to get dark, a sudden fear overwhelmed her that the men were in danger. Her friend assured her they were spending the night with friends on the mainland, but the woman's feeling of danger persisted. Hours went by, the temperature outside the little house dropped, and without power or telephones on the island, she felt helpless.

Finally, late in the evening, exhausted from frustration and worry, the woman prepared for bed. Then came yet another feeling of danger, one that begged her to stay awake and go down to the dock to search for her husband. However, fatigue won out and she collapsed on the bed, an action that was to cost her dearly in guilt and self-torture, for her husband and his friend both drowned in the channel that night.

Here in front of me several years later was this woman. Because of guilt, self-condemnation, and even anger at her husband for leaving her, the normal grieving process had been suppressed, and thus delayed. She had become depressed, losing her spark, her enthusiasm. All this became obvious during the session, so we worked together on her need to stay open, to allow room for whatever feelings might come to the surface and accept them as her teaching for the moment. She left that day determined to listen more to the feelings of her heart.

After a few months, she came to see me a second time. She looked more mature, as if she had become more grounded. This time it took very little prompting on my part for her tears to start flowing. Her grief and suffering were right on the surface, which to me was a most beautiful sign of strength and courage. Now we would work on a much deeper level, and that work had to start with her husband. While she was talking, a wonderful door was opened to allow more resolution on her grief. She had been looking at me, but now suddenly her eyes widened and her mouth opened in surprise.

"You look just like my husband. You didn't before. But now you do."

A long pause followed in silence, me holding as still as I could, praying for God's help within, and she obviously going through rapidly changing feelings and thoughts. She was speechless, and then sensed the presence of her husband telling her, "I love you. I don't blame you at all. Please forget the past, and accept what happened. Let go of then, and feel right now how deep our love is."

I shall never forget the peace that entered her face, still wet with tears, and the dancing sparkle of light in her eyes revealing the joy of understanding. This was a victory for her. She had overcome bitterness and self-pity. She had opened her heart to far

more than her husband. She leaned forward and hugged me, not as a woman hugging a man, but as a woman hugging her long-forgotten maleness. She was the picture of wholeness, of oneness, of reintegration which allows the Presence of God to flow through.

Without a doubt this woman will lose and regain this peace many times, but she will never be the same. She had seen past the separateness of life and death. Now, on her own, a whole new level of work had opened, making possible an awareness of the continuity of being. Although this woman was aware of many things, her husband's death had been final to her. He was completely gone. For her, there was no sense of the aliveness of their love, of the continuation of their relationship. This was complicated by her guilt about her shortcomings as a wife, and the anger directed at her husband for both leaving her emotionaly (the problem in their relationship) and physically (death). The glimpse in our session of his aliveness and forgiving love will now allow her to forgive him and also herself. If she remains sincere, forgiveness will allow the fullness of their love to be expressed, and love will enable her to see and feel the purpose, the divine intention, behind such a seeming tragedy.

Often, the death of a loved one is the stimulus which propels a person onto the spiritual path. This happened to a former neighbor some years ago. We were both new to the area, and had not become more acquainted than exchanging a passing hello whenever we saw this young couple out walking with their two little children.

While we were away on vacation, the young woman's husband was killed in a motorcycle accident. When we returned shortly after the incident, another neighbor called us to let us know what had happened. Knowing our background and work, she urged us to try to help this young woman. It was evening, and we were tired from a long drive, but we also hesitated to push ourselves on someone who probably was wanting to be left alone. We decided the best way to help was to inwardly send strength and love to both; to her in her grieving and to him in his transition. So I sat down in the living room to attempt this, while Joyce was in the bedroom. I was doing some stretches on the rug to try to loosen up my muscles, when I thought I heard someone calling me — a man's voice. What followed was an unmistakable feeling of the presence of this young man in the living room with me. I heard no more, but felt he was urging me to help his wife. I can't explain how I knew this. In fact, I wasn't even sure if all this was in my imagination, possibly aided by fatigue — but I couldn't ignore the experience.

I shared what had happened with Joyce, and we decided that I would walk down the hill to the woman's house. I would have preferred Joyce come with me, but Rami was a baby then and was sound asleep in her crib. I went alone. After a moment of doubt, wondering why I was there, I knocked on her door. She opened the door and welcomed me into the house, appearing composed as if nothing had happened. However, I could see she was still in a state of shock. I fully intended to withhold my experience from her, but once we had settled down into chairs, out it all came, just as it happened. Immediately she started crying, and I concluded I was being insensitive to her delicate condition. But no, she thanked me for coming, and said she had not allowed herself to cry. Still she was amazed. She had nothing in her conceptual framework to explain such an event. I told her a few stories of other experiences of death in a family, including a true story of a woman who persisted and finally was able to reach her husband and be assured of his nearness and love. This especially gave her hope.

The next day she asked to borrow any helpful books, and we gave her several. The one that helped her the most was White Eagle's *Sunrise.* Still later, she asked for help to pray and meditate, initially motivated by a burning desire to contact her husband. She became like a flower opening in the sun. Joyce and I sat with her, the three of us sending her husband love, enclosing him in light. That night he came to her in a dream (or rather she came to him). She woke up the next day wonderfully encouraged.

We spent quite some time with her in the weeks that followed. Some days a dark gloom would envelope her, the result of a doubting mind. She would then read, or pray, or work, and finally break through again. Prior to the death of her husband, both of them were uninterested in spiritual matters. They loved each other, but were quite absorbed in material living. The shock and pain of this experience opened this woman's heart to the deeper purpose of life, and literally catapulted her into the spiritual life. Now nothing made sense to her except learning to know God and gaining a deeper understanding of the meaning of life.

At one point in our relationship, our neighbor lamented that if only she and her husband had made the time to learn about these things before his passing, how much more prepared they both would have been. She longed to have devoted their lives togethe toward the spiritual aspects of life. So much of their time had been spent on earning a living, buying a house, and a thousand other "important" things.

An experience that has happened several times to Joyce and me has helped to make this point even clearer. Once when Joyce was away from home, I was sitting, "trying" to meditate and I went on a very interesting trip. I had the vivid image of Joyce dying in a car accident. Ordinarily I treat images like this as just part of my crazy, undisciplined mind, try to let them go, and continue with whatever process I was using. This time, however, I just let the scenario run its course, complete with all the feelings. I went through the shock, the profound feelings of loss. Tears were in my eyes as emptiness overwhelmed me. Everyone was notified, friends and family came for the funeral, but I just wanted to be alone. Soon I was, just me and my thoughts. But no! How absurd! Joyce was right here waiting for me to settle down and be with her in that place of peace within, where we've always met. With renewed determination I turned my attention within, breathed the gentlest of breaths, and there she was so beautiful to behold. There I was also, not just beholding her, but being the One who is both of us. A feeling of love pervaded everything.

This experience happened several other times in different ways to Joyce and me. Each time, the end result was a deep appreciation for each other, and for the privilege of sharing our lives and the spiritual journey together.

Those of you who have lost dear ones...although you may miss the physical presence, yet try to realize that something, a great gift, has been given to you. It is difficult to describe this gift, because it is of a spiritual nature. We might say it is a seed planted in your soul garden. This seed can grow into a lovely flower. Yes, we know that a physical loss can never be replaced, but still we say that a great and compensating blessing can come into your soul as a result of that loss, an increased understanding of your life. You may not have it yet, but it is coming. It takes a long time for this divine consciousness to develop and grow in the individual soul. Nevertheless this seed is sown and the flower of spiritual understanding is growing, until one day, when it is come into its full glory, you will wonder at its beauty.

WHITE EAGLE

In a deep love relationship, we must face the fear that one day our beloved may die before we do, and we would have to face the loneliness and emptiness. Everyone has this fear operating to some degree, whether consciously or unconsciously. For some people the fear is so great that they distance themselves from all people, thinking this is protecting them from some inevitable hurt. Unfortunately, each day then holds loneliness and emptiness.

When Barry was in psychiatry training we were involved in many different group sessions. In one encounter group session a woman angrily accused me of making a grave mistake with my life — that I was loving Barry too much. One day he would die, and then I would be sorry and have nothing. I was furious with this woman for saying such an awful thing. Then I realized she had touched an unconsious fear within me that was actually keeping me from loving Barry deeper. With the fear on the surface, I could now more easily work with it. As it turned out, I should have thanked this woman.

We all have probably known people who have lost a special animal. When asked if they would like another pet they often reply, "Oh no, never again. The pain was just too great when my pet died." On a subtle level the same holds true for human relationships. Perhaps you have experienced the death of a loved one as a child, or as an adult. If you remember this experience only in a painful way, you are likely to hold yourself back to some degree from really loving another person again.

A while ago I attended a workshop on grieving. I felt unresolved feelings about the death of our beloved dog Bokie. Of the thirty people in the workshop, I shall never forget one woman. She related how her husband had died four years previously of cancer. The day after his death she gave birth to their first son. Three and a half years later the little boy died of the same cancer. As she related her story we all held our breath. No one in the room had experienced the hand of death as strongly as this woman. But then she went on to tell us how grateful she was for even the brief contact with her husband and son. They had taught her so much that her experiences with them had been her main spiritual teachings. She felt her life had been completely changed for the better just because of knowing them, and now she was ready to love again. As she spoke, a beautiful light surrounded her, and every one in the room felt overwhelming love for her. She had found the courage to see past the darkness of death into the light by her continuous feeling of gratitude. You just knew this woman would feel much love in her future relationships.

With practiced faith we come to the realization that God is love, and sends death out of love, not punishment, and for the advancement of our soul. I have an elderly woman friend who had been married to her husband for fifty years when he developed terminal cancer. She lovingly nursed him at home through the final stages of his transition. When he died she sold their home and moved to a small apartment. There she placed just one picture of her husband where she could see it each morning. She told me that as the weeks, months, and years passed, she found she could feel the presence of her husband more and more. She said that in a way she felt closer to him now than she did all the fifty years of their marriage. Now she could feel his guiding and protecting essence always with her.

One week after our second daughter, Mira, was born, I felt strong enough to go for my first walk. It was the night of the full moon and everything seemed magical outside. I put Mira to sleep and asked Barry to come with me. He felt we couldn't leave such a new baby alone so he asked me to go by myself. I was out the door and down the driveway when an old fear hit me. Having been raised in a metropolitan area, I had acquired a hestitation to walk alone at night. I tried to talk myself into going since the night seemed so special. Looking into the dark woods, I listened to all the little ground animals scurrying about. I was afraid to go alone, yet I wanted to very much. Just then I felt a distinct rubbing sensation on my leg. I knew instantly it was the spirit of our dog Bokie who had died 10 months previously. He was letting me know he was there and would protect me every step of the way. What a splendid walk it was! *I knew then that we never walk alone after a loved one has passed on. They are by our side willing to help, if we can open to their presence.*

With true love there is no void after death unless we create it ourselves. Love does not go anywhere. As in the case of the elderly couple, love often increases after a spouse has passed on. If you are the one remaining in the body, you have the joy and anticipation of reunion. You can use each day to master yourself more deeply. When the day comes for your transition you will meet your beloved as radiantly beautiful as you possibly can be; much like the bride meeting her groom on their wedding day. In truth we are all both brides and grooms preparing ourselves for the wedding ceremony which will unite us with God, our Heavenly Beloved.

The ideal in a relationship is not to fear the death of a loved one, but to concentrate on the merging of our hearts. When death then comes, there can be no separation, for each lives on in the b

ing of the other. The loss of a partner's body does not end the relationship. It merely changes it. For the one in the spirit world, there is a new opportunity to expand in consciousness and thus shower down strength, love, and help upon one's earthly beloved. For the one remaining in the body, there is the challenge of keeping attuned to the spirit world — one foot in heaven and one foot on earth. By doing so, that partner can not only maintain a close feeling of the presence of their beloved, but also can become more ware of the Eternal Presence of God in their lives.

A television celebrity couple had lived sixty devoted years together. On the day his wife died the man felt loneliness. His human side grieved deeply over the loss. He missed his wife's body. That night he lay down in the same bed they had always slept in. Just before he drifted to sleep he felt the loving arms of his wife surround him and carry him to her new home. He knew then that death had not brought an end to their relationship. They were off on a new adventure together.

It is important that we allow ourselves to grieve over the loss of a partner. Much is learned from this essential process. It is equally important to celebrate our loved one's passing through the death initiation. With our love, support, and release, our partner is free to soar and thus help to lift us both.

The thought of our partner's death can bring us deeply into our hearts. *If we could live with the consciousness that our time together in physical bodies is limited, then our relationship could attain a deeper, fuller level.* To walk this earth hand-in-hand with our beloved is indeed a great blessing, one that can invoke in us deep gratitude. The Giver of life that gives us the love we feel for each other will sustain this love through all the initiations of life, especially after death, if we but ask and maintain our contact with the source of that love.

Love that ends is the shadow of love; true love is without beginning or end.

HAZRAT INAYAT KHAN

eighteen

The Shared Heart

A Story

Every soul has to withstand great pressure and to be well tested. Suppos-
ing the Master called upon you to do an important piece of work which
was going to involve many souls; and supposing you had not been tested
and proved? It is possible that you would break down under the stress of
the work. We are telling you this in order to help you in your endeavors
to follow the path of light, with all its testings and disappointments.

WHITE EAGLE

A man and woman climbed for hours up the great mountain. Starting in the new light of dawn, many times during the day their
bodies longed for rest. Hour after hour they pushed onward,
determined to carry out their Master's instructions. He had told
them this would be a higher initiation into the mystery of their love
together and they wanted this more than anything else in the
world. So many times in the past they had come close to feeling
their oneness, and tasting the ecstatic bliss of the mystical marriage. Today their deepest desires might be fulfilled.

As they climbed high on the mountain, the soil with its alpine vegetation had long since been replaced by rock. Sometimes they encountered slopes of loose rocks, sometimes massive boulders that could only be mounted with great effort, and sometimes sheer faces of granite that required careful attention for every step and handhold. They might have been better equipped, but the Master had spoken to their hearts, telling them to carry nothing on this journey — that their needs would be met.

During the late morning, the woman suddenly slipped on a treacherous rock face. Quickly the man grasped her hand while bracing himself against the mountain. Their knees turned rubbery with fear, so they sat together. Although she had almost lost her life, it was *his* eyes that now reflected doubt. Reading his unspoken thoughts, she took his hand in hers, and spoke softly.

"My beloved, sometimes what we are doing seems insane to me too, but we can't forget the Master's words to us, nor give up our journey after coming so far."

He looked deeply into the eyes he loved more than any other eyes in the world, and finally saw his real self reflected there. She saw that familiar spark rekindled in his eyes as he replied,

"And my beloved, even now I can feel unseen hands helping us, guiding our every step, protecting us from injury."

With their faith restored, a smile of trust formed together on their lips. They rose to continue their journey.

They had gone but a short distance when they found themselves on a level space at the top of one of the mountain's lesser peaks. The couple stopped and stood very still. They felt a certain inner prompting they had learned to trust over the years. This was the place! They looked at each other and knew. Not a word needed to be said.

The view was breathtaking. The valley sprawled out far below them, followed by range after range of mountains merging into the distant horizon. The wind blew strongly at times, but was warmed by the sun which was now high in its arcing path. The smells, the sights, the sounds of the wind, the rarified atmosphere, were all exhilarating to the couple.

They kneeled facing each other. Silently each thanked God for the opportunity given to them in this lifetime. With closed eyes, each reflected on the extraordinary events that had led them to this place and time. They thought about the many times they had almost given up, not only their marriage, but their spiritual quest as well.

Both reflected on a period of deepest despair, when their whole life as they had known it seemed to crumble into pieces. They had also knelt together then, and prayed their hearts out to the Lord of the universe for help. There on the floor reduced to complete helplessness, they learned a deep lesson of humility: that God, the spirit of love and wisdom, is the only true power there is. They knew in that moment that God alone is the doer, the thinker, the lover, that in fact, there is no existence except God. All that was left for them in that moment was to feel a boundless gratitude, which emerged from their attunement to the Divine Will.

As the couple continued meditating on the mountain, they remembered the wonderful experience that came next. The light of the room seemed to grow brighter and brighter. All sound stopped, just as if the sounds of life were coming from a record player, and someone lifted the needle off the record. The stillness in the room was unearthly! The light became so bright that all objects in the room disappeared. Yet, far from being blinding, it was soft, soothing, and seemed to also be a physical substance that penetrated their bodies, filling them with joy.

From the heart of that stillness, from the source of the radiance, indeed, from inside as much as outside of their beings, there emerged a voice more lovely than any they had ever heard. This voice was neither male nor female, and carried with it the most wonderful, delicate colors that could be felt as well as seen and heard. Yet, as extraordinary as all this was, and raised as they were in consciousness, the couple felt completely at ease as if this were a natural order of things.

This was their first contact with the Master. With great wisdom and love, he (or she) had spoken to them through their own divine natures. He revealed to them the purpose of their lives together, the training that would be necessary, and his role in helping them. He informed them that they would have to pass certain tests and prove their selflessness. When and if they did, they could help humanity reach a much higher degree of love. In the meantime, he would remain close, helping and guiding them. It would be up to them, however, to keep a loving stillness so they might be able to hear his voice, which would be identical to their own intuition.

The Master had communicated all this with only a few words that seemed instantaneous. When he finished speaking, the light in the room grew in intensity to a point where all seemed to be absorbed into it. Then the light subsided, and the couple embraced each other in thankfulness.

Time passed unnoticed as the two continued meditating on the mountain. Remembering the day of the Master's appearance seemed to draw them nearer to him. That had been the beginning. From that day on, they possessed a new strength and faith that would be tried to the utmost. Test after unbelievable test was given to them by some unseen but purposeful hand. Slowly and systematically, every flaw and weakness in their soul was brought to the surface to be bathed in their tears of forgiveness, dried by the sun-like warmth of true wisdom, and then transmuted into strengths by the Divine Alchemist.

Each year seemed like a lifetime, but gradually they learned to trust that inner voice, the voice of their Master. And so it finally happened, in what may have been a long time to some, the blink of an eye to others, that the woman and man received their final instructions from within: to leave their work, their money, their possessions, to leave everything behind and journey to a certain great mountain, where they would receive a higher initiation.

Now, on their mountain perch, some gentle force was urging them to look more deeply inside their souls. They both surrendered to this ingoing wave of energy. Holding still, their breathing changed to a slow and very refined rhythm. Their awareness was shifting inside, away from all that their senses were picking up, away from outer thoughts and feelings, away even from each other's physical presence. The gentle peace of the Spirit was carrying them each to a world much more vast than what they were used to. Scenes of beauty unequalled on earth began to open up before them both. Although separate, they each found themselves in what appeared to be a garden, with flowers and shrubs that scented the air with their glory. Before them both was a pool of what looked more like scintillating liquid light than water. On the far side of the pool stood a being whose brightness even surpassed the pool. The man and woman, although temporarily separated from each other, shared this same vision. Both knew at the same moment that this was their Master, their teacher, their guide. Both felt embraced by the love of this being, who seemed all love. Both also felt they were embracing all existence, that the Master, the garden the whole universe pulsated within them. Then, within each, a wondrous voice vibrated into form:

You have felt who I am, and have approached Me individually.
Now come to Me together. Have courage.

The garden dissolved, and the couple again felt their outer bodies and consciousness. The sun had passed its mid-point and the wind was strongly blowing. They opened their eyes and looked at each other, knowing they shared what had happened. They knew they could return to that heavenly garden and state as a couple, but how? They reached for each other's hands and looked deeply into each other's eyes, their breathing harmonizing into one breath.

Something strange was happening. Why this empty feeling inside, this feeling of being here and yet not being here? And what was this movement? The mountain seemed to be moving under them, accompanied by a low, deep rumbling. No, it was more of a groan...almost sounding human. They looked again at each other and the face of their beloved seemed somehow different. The mouth, the hair, the nose, even the eyes had a vaguely animal-like appearance. Was this projection, or was it actually happening? Each knew they should trust and allow it all to be, but despite their efforts a fear was mounting within them both.

The woman's face had by now become the face of a wild beast with crazed penetrating eyes. The man felt fear as never before. What demonic force was this? He started to close his eyes but they would not close. They were frozen open. He seemed paralyzed.

The groan was getting louder, changing into a deafening moan, but beyond the sound, from some faraway place, the man vaguely heard a word being repeated. At first indistinct, it became clearer: ''courage...courage...COURAGE...'' He latched onto that word and was given renewed strength. He prayed for courage. All of his being reached out and accepted courage, as if he was finally accepting a gift that he had refused many times in the past. Now possessing this gift, he could love this hideous face as yet another expression of God's creation. Slowly, the face shimmered and was transformed back into that of his beloved. A peaceful calm enveloped his soul, and the mountain as well.

Gazing at his beloved, he understood how she too had been tested and had overcome the same fear. Together they had learned to appreciate the power of their animal natures; the instinctual forces in the souls of men and women alike, controlled by the fear of death, killing to survive, and overcome only by the power of love.

The wind had now become a gentle breeze, and the warming sun was welcomed by the pair. Silently the woman prayed to the

All-Loving Spirit to unite her with her earthly beloved. The memory of the Master standing by the pool of light in the Heavenly Garden was burned into her soul. She understood his words:

You have felt who I am, and have approached Me individually.

She knew deeply the condition of heavenly bliss.

Now come to me together...come to me together. Have courage.

She needed to harmonize her whole being with her earthly beloved before she could truly unite with her Heavenly Beloved.

Resolving to do this, she looked deeply into the face that had become more of a home to her than any structure of wood or stone. He was so beautiful to behold, and was looking at her with great love. She felt as if his eyes were caressing her with the gentlest of touches, arousing in her waves of longing. Her body was coming alive with sensations so sweet she was surprised.

Now some magnetic force was drawing her eyes to his lips. Never had they looked more attractive. Invisible waves of bliss seemed to flow from his lips into every part of her body, flooding her with ecstatic sensations. She noticed he was nude...and she was too. When had they taken off their clothes? She looked at his body, alive and pulsing with attractiveness, and remembered their sweetest times of sexual union, when their bodies danced together as one body to the sublime rhythm only lovers know.

The presence of God and the master seemed especially close. Suddenly she was feeling shame and guilt, as if her nudity and desire were something evil. But the loving presence stayed close, as if to reassure her that nothing in the universe is inherently evil...that only our thinking makes it so. Shame and guilt are but conditions of the human mind holding itself separate from the creator of the mind.

She again relaxed, and now the attractive pull from his lips and body was overwhelming. Ripples of energy were drawing their lips together. Giving in to this force, her lips met his, and her body nearly exploded with rapture. Never had she experienced a kiss like this! Never had she felt so much joy in her body. Powerful forces now seemed to be pulling on her in different ways, and she felt she was losing consciousness. Amid intense pleasure, she found she was gasping for breath. Some deeply pungent odor appeared to be suffocating her. She felt desperate for air, yet she was helplessly trapped in some great momentum of energy. Her body felt like some massive planet spinning and hurtling through space...toward what?

Terrified, with tears streaming down her face, she started to ask her beloved for help but was stopped by some invisible force. She called out with all her heart to God, her Heavenly Father and Mother. Then, gradually, her breath started to return and her mind clear. Little by little, her heart was filling with a desire for God, for *more than physical* love. As this was happening, the overwhelming forces in her body seemed to change; not disappearing but rather softening and expanding outward. Then she understood. She had let her longing for the heavenly condition become focused only in her body, which then operated with a consciousness of its own. Now her passion, even her sexual desire, filled every part of her...body, mind, and heart...with desire for the One Spirit. This was the secret of transmutation of sexual energy — how it could be spiritualized. Seeing the light in her beloved's eyes, she realized he too had understood the test they had both passed through.

Finding themselves still on the mountain, the couple noticed that the shadows were lengthening as the sun neared the horizon. A hush and stillness came over the mountain, as if it too had gone through some great initiation, passing its own test.

The man and woman were still kneeling in front of each other on their rocky perch. Hours had passed without food or water, yet they felt rested and replenished. Not knowing what else was in store for them, they continued praying and meditating, asking God for strength and courage for whatever lay ahead. After a while they sensed the beckoning presence of the Master and abandoned themselves to his emanations of love and wisdom. Suddenly they seemed to be rising, guided by his unseen but warmly protective presence. Both felt deep appreciation and gratitude to this One who was the epitome of selflessness, never wavering in his protection of them.

The air around them stirred and was changing. Scenes were opening up around them. Intuitively, the couple felt they were transiting into what could become their future. The scenes were becoming more and more real. Their consciousness was entering fully into their surroundings as though drifting into a living dream. The moment before the transition was complete, the couple sensed an approaching great test and prayed for help...

They found themselves in a room or hall, surrounded by a number of people, each looking to them for inspiration and guidance. Both took turns clothing the eternal wisdom of being into words that seemed to carry with them a healing presence to those listening. The woman and man were aware of the impact of their words, for some people were in tears, some were smiling radiantly, and some were looking at them reverently. Seeing this, they would reveal that they were no different than anyone else in the room, that two persons used by God to speak was no different than God's using others to hear. Only God, the Source of all being, should be worshipped.

Days merged into weeks, and weeks into months. The couple continued teaching, healing, and inspiring. Although they often prayed to stay humble, a subtle change began to overcome them. In their sincere desire to serve they had always noticed the needs of the people around them. Now, imperceptibly, they started serving the needs of the individuals rather than heeding the Impersonal Voice within them. It was all very subtle at first, for the individuals thus treated seemed much happier than those treated with impersonal love and truth. Furthermore, this change began attracting many more persons. Ever so slightly, another change took place in the couple. Increasingly they saw themselves as different, and then, even as special. Their whole consciousness gradually shifted from the inner to the outer world. Their words no longer carried the power, the magic. One after another of their followers felt alienated. The couple even started arguing with each other. They were losing their harmony.

One evening in a rare moment away from everyone, the two sensed something was very wrong. Throwing off the false-pride that had entered their lives, they admitted to each other deep feelings of sadness. Both realized they had stopped reaching out to one another, had almost ceased communicating. Now some invisible floodgate opened, and they saw their great mistake. Through their tears, they saw how they had misused divine power. They had, as individuals, been taking credit for God's work. As channels of God's love, they had forgotten the origin of that love. The flutes, hearing their sweet music, forgot to acknowledge the One whose lips blew so gently through them.

Now they felt the strength and force of fame and power, yet at the same time how very empty and meaningless they were. As if for the first time, they knew what it means to do the work of the Heavenly Mother and Father, to unquestionably follow the inner guidance regardless of personal outcome, whether theirs or anyone else's. With awe and gratitude, they felt as if they stood on the brink of a momentous discovery. Never had they fully realized what true humility was. The words, *"Not my will but thine, oh Lord,"* were vibrating deeply within their hearts, becoming an inseparable part of their beings. With this came a freedom they had never known. It mattered not whether they taught with their words to great multitudes or with their beings to the trees and flowers. What they did in the world was no more important than who they were, or what they thought and felt. This had been a most important initiation.

The couple looked long and deeply into each other's eyes. No longer were these the eyes of another person. No longer were there two persons. From perfect humility, perfect love was born, and out of this love came Oneness. With a feeling that embraced all feelings and yet transcended them all, the Divine Presence was both seeing itself and being seen.

Absorbed in this state for some time, they now realized they were back on the mountain, glowing in the rainbow colors of the sunset. The presence of the Master was with them once again. At this magical time of day, when all of nature seems to reveal the sacred peace of the Divine Presence, this being of light, this servant of servants, was again in their midst. This time, however, his presence was awesome, his power and love overwhelming. His beautiful voice rang out in both their hearts:

The three tests you have passed today on this mountain, representing the three lower psychic centers of being, prove your dedication to serving God. Had any selfishness remained during even one of these initiations, you would have surely failed.

Few couples choose to undertake the journey you have chosen together, and very few of those learn the joy of self-sacrifice. Most couples desire the bliss of the shared heart, the ecstacy of union, but the two of you have gone deeper. You are among the very few who have given up the pleasures of the senses in your desire to serve humanity. Yet what you have given up you now possess. When you learned the lesson of complete humility, your relationship attained a oneness which you now feel. The secret, which you both knew all along in your hearts but had to experience more deeply, was unconditional service; giving of yourselves without reward or recognition. This is identical to unconditional love, for love is service, and service is love.

The experiences you passed through today were creations of your own minds and feelings, but they were no less real because of this. Understand that you can never be tested by some outer force or circumstances. All initiations of the soul are the domain of the Presence of God within us. These tests are allowed for our development, and only when we are ready.

Passing the first two tests today demonstrated your readiness for the third, which very few pass together as a couple. As you can feel, the very earth around you is tingling with joy and happiness, for there is a service, a gift of love, that can only be given when an earthly woman and man together overcome the projection of their lower natures upon each other, and live and feel as one being.

The two of you are a reflection of each other, the One God masquerading as two bodies, two minds, two hearts, perfectly complementary to each other. Now possessing this secret, and living your life simply and humbly, your inner joy will inspire many. Your love and devotion to the Great Spirit within you will silently heal the bitterness and resentment in the hearts of those you contact. In truth, your very beings and mastery as an earthly couple will have a profound impact on the vibrations of the earth itself. And you, my dear children, will hardly notice any of this, so absorbed will you be in joyfully serving God's Plan. Your uniting with your earthly beloved has united you with your Heavenly Beloved.

We are now inseparable. Peace be with you.

The couple rose to their feet. The last glow of the sunset bathed the mountain in a delicate violet-purple light, the color of more-than-human love. Turning away from the mountain, they watched the full moon emerge from its dazzling white aura on the horizon, as if the distant hills were giving birth to this globe of light. With hearts overflowing with thankfulness, the couple joined hands in preparation for their journey. At that moment, they knew their whole destiny was being born and, like the brilliant moon, would provide light for each step down the mountain and every step for all time.

In the union of two loving hearts is the Unity of God.

HAZRAT INAYAT KHAN

About the authors:

Barry and Joyce Vissell have counseled individuals and couples, and led groups, classes and workshops since 1972. They have lived near Santa Cruz, California, since 1975.

They are available for workshops and events, and should be contacted through:

Ramira Publishing
P.O. Box 1707
Aptos, Ca. 95001

Copies of this book may be ordered from:

Ramira Publishing
P.O. Box 1707
Aptos, Ca. 95001

Send $8.95   (postage and handling included;
              outside U.S.A., add $1.00)
California residents include $.58 tax (total $9.53)

INDEX